PUBLIC MANAGEMENT
DEVELOPMENTS

UPDATE 1992

ORGANISATION FOR ECONOMIC CO-OPERATION AND DEVELOPMENT

ORGANISATION FOR ECONOMIC CO-OPERATION AND DEVELOPMENT

Pursuant to Article 1 of the Convention signed in Paris on 14th December 1960, and which came into force on 30th September 1961, the Organisation for Economic Co-operation and Development (OECD) shall promote policies designed:

— to achieve the highest sustainable economic growth and employment and a rising standard of living in Member countries, while maintaining financial stability, and thus to contribute to the development of the world economy;

— to contribute to sound economic expansion in Member as well as non-member countries in the process of economic development; and

— to contribute to the expansion of world trade on a multilateral, non-discriminatory basis in accordance with international obligations.

The original Member countries of the OECD are Austria, Belgium, Canada, Denmark, France, Germany, Greece, Iceland, Ireland, Italy, Luxembourg, the Netherlands, Norway, Portugal, Spain, Sweden, Switzerland, Turkey, the United Kingdom and the United States. The following countries became Members subsequently through accession at the dates indicated hereafter: Japan (28th April 1964), Finland (28th January 1969), Australia (7th June 1971) and New Zealand (29th May 1973). The Commission of the European Communities takes part in the work of the OECD (Article 13 of the OECD Convention). Yugoslavia has a special status at OECD (agreement of 28th October 1961).

Publié en français sous le titre :

ÉVOLUTIONS DANS LA GESTION PUBLIQUE :
MISE A JOUR 1992

FOREWORD

This report is the second update of *Public Management Developments: Survey – 1990* (OECD, Paris, 1990). It reflects developments in public sector management in Member countries as reported by them at the end of 1991.

The report has been compiled by David Rushforth of the OECD Secretariat in close collaboration with the network of national correspondents designated by Member countries for this purpose (see Annex). At its meeting on 12-13 March 1992, the Public Management Committee recommended that the report be made available to the public. It is published on the responsibility of the Secretary-General.

CONTENTS

PREFACE

This series of reports is produced by the OECD Public Management Committee. It is designed to respond to the growing demand in both Member and non-Member countries for up-to-date information on policies, programmes and measures for improving the efficiency and effectiveness of public sector management, and on the institutions responsible for developing and implementing them. These reports put into a succinct and easily accessible form a large amount of dispersed information on what has been recognised as an important area of structural adjustment policy.

This report, as its name implies, is an update of the information contained in previous publications in the series, i.e. the 1990 survey and its 1991 update. It should, therefore, be read in association with those two publications which provide the context for many of the initiatives mentioned. For this reason the format remains similar: a set of country summaries provided by national correspondents together with a list of those contacts. A difference in this year's report is that the statistical tables have not been included. Instead, ''factsheets'' aimed at facilitating the identification of trends across time and countries summarise the principal recent public management developments in each country together with the key institutions responsible for improvements. An introductory summary of developments has been added to illustrate main directions taken during 1991.

INTRODUCTION

Correspondents from 23 Member countries have contributed to this report, which summarises the public sector reform initiatives undertaken by governments of OECD Member countries during 1991. This introduction provides a résumé of some of the main initiatives reported by countries in this latest Update. The examples included here are indicative of trends, but of course they are neither entirely representative of the full range of reforms nor of the many nuances reported in the country chapters.

Reform programmes

In several countries there was a comprehensive re-assessment of priorities on the public sector reform agenda as a result of a change in government. Thus in **Finland,** the new Government has set as its public management priorities: effectiveness, productivity, decentralisation and reform of central government guidance, all with the overall objective of improving the quality of public services. In **New Zealand,** restructuring of the public sector has continued under the new Government but with, in particular, major changes to social policy leading to significant consequential organisational changes. And in **Sweden** the economic policy of the new coalition Government includes efforts to renew and limit the public sector with the aim of restricting public expenditure, extending the use of market mechanisms and focussing public management on the setting of targets, clearly specifying required results and analysing and evaluating those results.

Other countries have also reported overall reviews of their approach to public sector management. Thus, for example, in **Canada** a new concept, the "Shared Management Agenda" was introduced as a collaborative approach (between the Deputy Minister of a department, and the Secretary of the Treasury Board and the Comptroller General) to identifying and resolving larger management issues in the Public Service. In **Denmark** the Government submitted a report on the Modernisation Programme which identified a new pattern of problem-solving and management expected to emerge in the 1990s and which will be characterised by "placing citizens in the centre with better and cheaper solutions enabling a lower burden of taxation". In **Greece,** the public sector was redefined and provisions were made for the modernisation of the public administration (including the upgrading of public personnel) in important new legislation. In **Ireland** a new comprehensive agreement was signed by the Government and the social partners; the programme provides a strategic framework for the next decade with specific proposals which include fundamental structural reforms. In **Italy** a global strategy was launched which strengthened the integration and co-ordination of civil service issues within the national system. In the **Netherlands,** the three major drives during the 1990s will be towards "normalisation" of civil service conditions of employment (i.e. aligning them more with private sector practice), decentralisation, and greater efficiency; the slogan of the Government is "Fewer civil servants but a better service". In **Spain** the Government was reshaped and a number of ministries were restructured with the two basic aims of progressively introducing modernisation measures into the administration and adjusting central government to the challenges of the Single European Market in 1993. And in the **United Kingdom,** the restructuring of the civil service based on the "Next Steps" initiative continued.

Implementing reform programmes

Several countries reported the setting up of new high-level groups to lead and evaluate administrative reform programmes. For example, in **Austria** a team comprising the Minister of

Federalism and Administrative Reform, the Minister of Finance, and the Secretaries of State for Finance and for Personnel Administration now meets regularly to decide priorities and evaluate progress. In **Finland** the new Government has set up a permanent Ministerial Committee to guide and monitor the reform process. And in **Spain** a "Government Agreement" proposed by the Minister for Public Administration binds all ministries to develop specific modernisation schemes under the guidance of two committees, one chaired by the Vice-President of the Government and the other by the Minister for Public Administration.

Evaluation

While still patchy, there is some evidence of progress towards more widespread evaluation of reform initiatives. Thus, for example, in **Australia** the Department of Finance is evaluating estimates practices; and the Financial Management Improvement Programme is being assessed by independent evaluators from outside the Department. In **Japan** the Prime Minister requested the third Provisional Council for the Promotion of Administrative Reform to examine, among other things, progress with the reforms, and several reports have been submitted. In **New Zealand,** a major review of the State sector reforms requested by the Minister of State Services was completed. In **Portugal,** there was an evaluation of the public administration salary system. And in the **United Kingdom,** the second review of the "Next Steps" Agencies was published.

There were also numerous efforts at policy and programme evaluation. For example, in **France,** the Interministerial Committee on Evaluation selected five areas of public policy for evaluation, and five other areas are being considered – one of which, government social policy, has already been approved by the Scientific Committee on Evaluation. In **Switzerland,** the investigations of the working party on legislative evaluation were completed. And the **United States** reported that there is continued strong support for the production of sound and timely programme evaluations.

Organisational and structural change

Two predominant types of broad restructuring emerge from the contributions received: those concerned to redistribute responsibilities between different levels of government; and those seeking to create more market-oriented operating conditions for specific government bodies. Examples of the former category include **Belgium,** where a Royal Decree was issued transferring to the Communities and Regions powers which include establishing the conditions of service of their staff, and **Finland,** where new legislation has been presented to Parliament to increase the self-government and economic responsibility of municipalities. In **France** a draft law was put before Parliament aiming to redefine the role of the central civil service vis-à-vis regional and local administration, and proposing new forms of co-operation between regional and local authorities. In **Japan** a bill on devolution of authority to local governments was enacted. In the **Netherlands** several central government tasks are to be given to municipalities, provinces and regional bodies leading to estimated savings of Gld 500 million. And in **Sweden** a new Local Government Act gives municipalities and county councils extensive new liberty to design and modify their own structures according to local conditions.

Other countries have changed the status of bodies on the boundaries with the private sector. Examples include **Austria** where new legislation transferred some tasks from ministries to private firms, and even provided for some administrative powers such as the issue of certain permits to be entrusted to private enterprise; **Belgium** where an act was passed to change the status of some public enterprises, thereby giving them more managerial freedom and allowing them to bring in private capital while affirming their public character; and **Canada** where nine new "Special Operating Agencies" were announced. In **France** the transformation of the Posts and Telecommunications into two public establishments was completed, and in the **United Kingdom,** 46 major businesses have now been privatised.

Restructuring of responsibility for administrative matters has also taken place, most notably in **Sweden** where changes include placing central matters of public administration with the Ministry of Finance, while leaving responsibility for regional and local administration, community development and the protection of consumer interests with the Ministry of Public Administration. The Cabinet Office's role in political co-ordination has also been reinforced. In **Germany** the Federal Government decided that of the eighteen current federal ministries, ten shall move to Berlin and eight will remain in Bonn.

Management of human resources

This remains an area attracting much attention in all Member countries and a field in which many comprehensive strategies as well as specific innovations are being implemented. The latter range from changing recruitment procedures and the conditions of employment of civil servants, to re-examining their pension schemes. In particular, many countries continue to examine ways of making public sector pay systems more flexible. In **New Zealand,** performance-based pay regimes have been operating since 1988 with the establishment of a system of ranges of rates for remuneration, but some concern has been expressed about resulting problems of wage drift and administrative complexity. In **Norway,** a new pay system has been implemented which permits positions at the same level to have different salary alternatives depending upon performance and other factors. In **Switzerland,** new legislation was introduced to allow "due account to be taken of the performance of the civil servant". In the **United Kingdom,** the Government is in the process of renegotiating most civil service pay agreements, one aim of which is to provide a more direct and regular link between individuals' pay and their performance. And in the **United States,** a new act was implemented which includes amongst its major features a requirement to develop and institute systems that strengthen the link between pay and performance.

Management development moved ahead on many fronts in numerous countries. In **Australia,** an appropriation of $A 10 million per annum for three years was approved to enhance the management skills and development of middle managers. In **Canada,** a special fund of $C 10 million has been set aside to support new departmental training initiatives. In **France,** as a move to ensure that training is tailored as closely as possible to needs, interministerial block appropriations for training will be decentralised to the regional Prefects. In **Ireland,** an initiative towards a more coherent approach to staff training and development was endorsed, staff development plans and training programmes based on needs surveys are to be promoted, and guidelines on best training practices are being prepared. In **Luxembourg,** a proposal to completely restructure the professional training currently offered by the Institute of Administrative Training is being debated by the Council of Ministers. And in the **Netherlands,** mobility is again being encouraged as a facet of management development.

Special attention continues to be given to the ranks of senior executives in many public services. In **Australia,** for example, the Government made a major statement on the role and training of senior management. In **Finland,** a special management training programme was started for approximately 100 top civil servants to increase, for example, their commitment to the changes needed in the public sector. And in **Norway,** 450 senior managers are to have their salaries and working conditions regulated by individual agreements which will permit their remuneration to be better related to performance. On the other hand, in **Canada,** the latest budget introduced a freeze on the performance pay of members of the management category.

Reducing the size of the administration

In a few countries, there are explicit efforts to reduce personnel numbers. These are: **Finland** where a new decision as part of the budget for 1992 and the financial frames for 1992-95 aims to reduce the number of posts in state administration by 5 per cent by 1995, in addition to previously announced cuts; **Japan** where the eighth personnel reduction plan was decided with the target for the five years from financial year 1992 of cuts by 4.52 per cent of total central goverment staff; and the **Netherlands** where a reduction of about 9 000 jobs in the central administration is targeted by 1994 in the "greater efficiency operation".

Managing for results

The contributions clearly demonstrate that the multi-faceted approach to making public sector management more efficient and effective, which was identified in previous reports, has continued. The reform agenda in Member countries has again devoted particular attention to ways of placing more emphasis on results. This is particularly well demonstrated in the Nordic countries. Thus, in **Finland,** a more result-oriented budget structure is being introduced for government agencies, and the Public Management Department of the Ministry of Finance was re-organised according to result-targeted projects instead of the more traditional office structure. In **Norway,** the overall public management reform strategy of the Ministry of Labour and Government Administration pays "special attention to performance-oriented and result-oriented management". In **Sweden,** management by results is now seen as fundamental to the budget process. Another example is **France,** where experiments with "centres of accountability" favour negotiation of the means needed for achieving objectives (which are also negotiated) rather than the application of pre-determined procedures – illustrating a shift from emphasis on tasks to achievement of goals.

This consistent concern with performance in the public sector has more than ever put the spotlight on the role and status of agencies. Thus in **Denmark** there is experimentation with "free agencies" in which more managerial freedom will be given and, in return, demands for results will be increased. Similarly, in the **Netherlands**"agencies are considered to be ideally suited for ensuring that the emphasis is shifted from resource-oriented authorisation to performance-oriented accountability". The **United Kingdom** cites a report by the Prime Minister's Efficiency Unit which recommends that "chief executives should be given greater authority and freedom in managing their agencies, including the ability to shop around for support services".

Financial management

Various moves towards giving government bodies a more commercial orientation by modifying their accounting systems have been reported by numerous countries. **New Zealand** continues to be at the forefront of much of this experimentation and reports that 1991/92 will be the first financial year when all departments will have had a full year on the new accrual accounting systems and reporting on outputs. Other examples include **Australia** where full accrual accounting is being introduced into the Department of Administrative Services which now charges market-based fees for its services aimed at recovering costs and allowing a margin for profit; and where the National Audit Office will start to charge full cost recovery for auditing financial statements from 1991/92. In **Austria** a pilot project in the Ministry of Public Economy and Transport is examining the use of cost accounting as a means of improving cost efficiency so as to establish the best balance between administrative costs and charges to clients. In the **Netherlands** the Government adopted the recommendations of a working group which included proposals for giving agencies the possibility of combining accrual accounting and commercial bookkeeping. And in **Sweden** the new Government strategy seeks to extend the use of market mechanisms and includes a model with frames for administrative costs of agencies aimed at giving them a clearer responsibility for costs.

In a similar vein, moves are reported towards more cost-effective property management in the public sector. For example, **Austria** has examined the use of buildings by the central federal administration and explored the notion that ministries should pay rents to the Ministry of Finance for the use of the buildings they occupy based on current market prices; and in **Norway,** budgetary reforms include modernisation of public property management involving the introduction of rent payments by user institutions and the transformation of the Directorate of Public Construction and Property into a public enterprise.

Multi-year budgeting is being extended in, for example, **Denmark,** where agreements on budget frameworks for a four-year period are an important element in the contracts for several of the new ''free agencies''; and in **Ireland,** where three-year administrative budgets for the period 1991-93 were introduced in most departments of the civil service.

Management of regulations

Several countries report specific initiatives in this domain, including **Greece,** where a committee has been established for the simplification of legislation and of other administrative acts; the **Netherlands,** where the Minister of Justice presented a paper to Parliament indicating how, amongst other things, laws can be made more consistent; **Sweden,** where work in regulatory reform continues, especially to speed up deregulation and to reduce the number of regulations in force by taking full advantage of computerised data bases; and **Turkey,** where over 1 000 measures to reduce bureaucratic formalities have now been implemented.

Service quality and client satisfaction

In a number of countries, significant new initiatives were undertaken to strengthen the notion of the public sector providing quality services for its clients. The most notable example was perhaps that of the **United Kingdom** where the ''Citizen's Charter'' was published with a focus on quality, choice, standards, and value-for-money within the nation's tax bill. A subsequent White Paper, ''Competing for Quality'', described steps to make it easier for the private sector to compete in providing services to all levels of government. In **Canada** an *ad hoc* committee on service standards was set up to help departments see if existing service standards meet client expectations and to develop new ones. A range of initiatives aimed at making the administration more responsive to its clients were also reported in the following countries: **Belgium, Denmark, Finland, France, Greece, Japan,** the **Netherlands, Portugal, Spain, Turkey,** and the **United States.**

AUSTRALIA

Organisational and structural change

In May 1991, the Minister for Industrial Relations announced that **workplace bargaining** had been endorsed for Australian Government employment and that demonstrable productivity improvement would be a feature of wage setting in the Australian Public Service (APS). A Secretaries' Committee, made up of the heads of eight public service agencies, has been set up and will prepare a discussion paper addressing a range of issues for implementing workplace bargaining. The advice of the Secretaries' Committee will be complemented by a group of three academics who will provide views on the same range of issues.

The **Joint APS Training Council** (JAPSTC), a joint advisory body with managers and unions and representatives from the education sector, was established in 1990. The role of the Council is to advise on Structural Efficiency Principle (SEP)-related training issues, that is, existing and future skills requirements, skills recognition and training to support award restructuring and improved efficiency in the APS. The Council is undertaking a number of projects to identify competencies for all major employment groups in the APS. These competencies will be used as the basis for training and development aimed at improving the employment-related skills of staff.

The Department of Administrative Services (DAS) is implementing a range of **common service reforms,** focusing its activities on client needs. Regulation of service use has been devolved to agencies. The DAS has been restructured to reflect this new focus and full accrual accounting is being introduced. Eighty-five per cent of DAS staff are now employed in commercialised areas of the organisation. Fees for services are market-based, aimed at recovering costs and allowing a margin for profit, and half DAS' revenue comes from businesses open to actual or potential competition. This is expected to rise to 90 per cent by 1993.

Financial management

The annual review of the "**Guidelines for Financial Statements of Commonwealth Entities**" has resulted in the publication of revised guidelines. Parallel guidelines for financial reporting by Commonwealth departments have also been revised and have enhanced disclosure requirements. The Australian National Audit Office (ANAO) will charge full cost recovery for the audit of financial statements from 1991/92.

The Department of Finance is working towards preparing its own financial statements on an accrual basis. This will assist in the Department's understanding of the benefits and costs of this accounting method. In order to provide a forum for discussion and advice on proposed revisions to financial statements guidelines, the Department of Finance set up two advisory panels of representatives from Commonwealth agencies. The ANAO and the Australian Society of Certified Practising Accountants are also represented on each panel. The process has worked well. Other discussion and educational activities on a range of matters are offered by the Department and it has also prepared a *Commonwealth Financial Management Handbook.*

The Department of Finance has prepared a set of proposals for the revision of the Audit Act. They aim to enhance accountability in terms of external financial reporting.

Staff management

The Australian Government made a major statement on the role and training of senior management in the APS in its response to a Senate Committee report. The Government supported the report's findings that the concept of the **Senior Executive Service** (SES) as a unified cohesive senior management group remained valid. However, it felt that the report's calls for greater centralised control of SES selection, deployment and development were neither appropriate nor practical in the current devolved management climate. Instead, it undertook to develop policies, guidelines and programmes which will provide improved career management and development strategies and opportunities for the SES. Specific initiatives were announced.

Performance appraisal schemes for the SES are intended to form the basis of performance pay arrangements. Agreement has also been reached with unions to introduce performance appraisal and pay for the Senior Officer Structure, which is the major sub-SES middle management group. The introduction of performance pay remains subject to endorsement by the Industrial Relations Commission, which has agreed in principle.

The Australian Government has approved an appropriation of A$ 10 million per annum for three years (1990/91 to 1992/93) to enhance the management skills and development of middle managers in the APS. The **Middle Management Development Programme** (MMDP) complements other structural, budgetary and administrative reforms designed to move the APS away from a bureaucratic administrative style to a strategic management style focusing on objectives, results, and relevance to the client.

During 1991, work continued on the reform of all major APS **classification structures.** Through the JAPSTC, particular emphasis was placed on identifying the skills and competencies necessary for staff in the new structures to undertake a wider range of tasks. The *1990 Survey of Human Resource Development* has been published and widely distributed.

New **selection and entry-level arrangements** for clerical staff have been introduced. Traditionally, entry to base-level clerical positions has been based solely on an applicant's performance on a range of aptitude tests. But, now, the nature of the applicant population and the type of work performed by lower-level clerical staff has changed. These arrangements still include a series of aptitude tests as the first part of the process. However, where appropriate, managers can now specify additional criteria relevant to the job. These additional selection criteria are then used in matching applicants to jobs or are assessed at interview. Applicants are referred for an interview in order of merit based on test scores.

Management of policy-making

In July 1990, the then Prime Minister announced his intention to consider **Commonwealth-State relations.** This initiative, which is supported by a Commonwealth-State Relations Secretariat (in the Department of the Prime Minister and Cabinet), involves the three levels of government in Australia working together to identify practical steps to achieve better co-operation within the framework of the Australian Constitution.

Heads of Government have also agreed that, in addition to the annual Financial Premiers' Conference, there will be at least one Premiers' Conference each year to deal with other matters, and that the Secretariat would have responsibility for co-ordinating arrangements for prior consultation with the States when decisions of the Commonwealth would impact directly on State finances.

Better quality service delivery and client satisfaction

In the 1970s, the need was recognised to ensure that immigrants had fair access to, and a fair share of, mainstream government services. Commonwealth agencies are now required to produce a second three-year **Access and Equity Plan** for the period 1991-94 that reflects the wider scope of the Access and Equity Strategy as it has developed. The emphasis on the double disadvantage faced by women has continued.

Regulatory review and reform

In 1991, the Department of the Prime Minister and Cabinet launched comprehensively revised and expanded guidelines for preparing departmental annual reports. These addressed a number of issues raised by Parliamentary committees in previous years.

Monitoring and evaluation

In March 1991, a Taskforce was set up in the Department of the Prime Minister and Cabinet to evaluate the **Access and Equity Strategy.** It will report as part of the 1992/93 budget process. The same Department is also co-ordinating a working group to discuss evaluating policy advice.

Estimates practices are being evaluated by the Department of Finance. The **Financial Management Improvement Programme** (FMIP) evaluation, for report in 1992, is also under way and is being conducted by independent evaluators from outside the Department of Finance. It will include an evaluation of the evaluation strategy.

In 1991, the Australian National Audit Office completed the first stage of an **efficiency audit** of the implementation of programme evaluation. It also completed part of the second stage of the audit of evaluation in preparation of the Budget.

FACTSHEET: AUSTRALIA

A.   PRINCIPAL RECENT PUBLIC MANAGEMENT DEVELOPMENTS

1983:
- Government discussion paper "Reforming the Australian Public Service" sets policy goals and leads to amendment of the Public Service Act.

1984:
- Government publishes "Budget Reform", a statement of achievements and intentions in reforming Australian Government financial administration.
- Financial Management Improvement Programme (FMIP) introduced as a major vehicle for linking expenditure control and better value for money.

1985:
- Access and Equity Programme introduced and Merit Protection and Review Agency set up.

1986:
- 1986 (first) review of the FMIP published.

1987:
- Machinery of government restructured:
  - number of departments reduced from 28 to 18;
  - Public Service Board abolished;
  - Public Service Commission set up;
  - most operational aspects of personnel management devolved to departments;
  - Efficiency Scrutiny Unit established; and
  - Government Business Enterprises reformed.
- Management Advisory Board (MAB) set up.
- Revised "Guidelines on Official Conduct of Commonwealth Public Servants" introduced.

1988:
- FMIP Progress (second) Report published.
- Programme Management and Budgeting implemented in all departments.
- New wage Agreement reached based on Structural Efficiency Principle.

1989:
- Management Improvement Advisory Committee (MIAC) set up.
- Further Steps Forward Strategy announced to accelerate Equal Employment Opportunity practices.
- Access and Equity Strategy extended.
- Performance Appraisal Programme for the Senior Executive Service introduced.
- Discussion paper, "APS 2000", examines the Australian Public Service workforce of the future.
- Revised regulations on purchasing to reduce the regulation of the purchasing process, with value for money as the main objective.

1990:
- FMIP evaluated by a Parliamentary Committee and report (third report, "Not Dollars Alone") published.
- Joint APS Training Council set up.
- Guidelines introduced for appraising the performance of Senior Executive officers.
- Purchasing Development Centre set up to train in purchasing.
- Social Justice Strategy implemented.
- Centralisation (with the Federal Government) of a national scheme of companies, securities and futures regulation.

1991:
- MAB/MIAC launch publication series.
- Secretaries' Committee (eight heads of agency) releases paper on improving APS productivity.
- Department of Administrative Services releases code for handling conflict of interest.
- Access and Equity Strategy evaluated.

B.   INSTITUTIONAL RESPONSIBILITY FOR PUBLIC MANAGEMENT IMPROVEMENT

ORGANISATION	TASKS AND RESPONSIBILITIES	OTHER INFORMATION
Department of Finance (DOF)	– Financial Management Improvement Programme (FMIP): Co-ordinator – Programme Management and Budgeting (PMB)	
Public Service Commission (PSC)	– policy aspects of recruitment, promotion, transfer, mobility, discipline and retirement of public personnel	A small independent statutory body. The former Public Service Board was abolished in 1987 and most operational aspects of personnel matters were devolved to individual departments. The heads of the DOF, the PSC and the DIR are members of the Management Advisory Board (MAB).
Department of Industrial Relations (DIR)	– industrial relations issues	
Department of the Prime Minister and Cabinet (PM&C) – Government Division – Corporate Services Division	– advice to Prime Minister and Minister Assisting Prime Minister for Public Service Matters on public service issues – responsibility for some aspects of administering Public Service Act 1992 – general responsibility for machinery of government – support to Secretary of the Department as chairperson of MAB – secretariat support to MAB	

AUSTRIA

Public management reform in Austria in 1991 included significant progress in the **Administrative Management Project.** This work, which was launched in 1989 on the basis of a decision of the Council of Ministers, is being developed by the Federal Chancellery.

The two inter-departmental study groups set up as a result of evaluation at the end of Phase One finished their work. The report of the "Management and Personnel" group was submitted to the government in May 1991 and that on "Budgeting and Controlling" is currently being finalised. On 8 October 1991, the Council of Ministers decided to change the process for the implementation phase of the project by placing responsibility in the hands of a government team comprising the Minister of Federalism and Administrative Reform, the Minister of Finance, and the Secretaries of State for Finance and for Personnel Administration. This group meets regularly to decide, on a step-by-step basis, the priorities for implementing the project by fixing deadlines for progress and evaluating results. This approach is necessary given that the Minister of Federalism and Administrative Reform is a minister within the Chancellor's Office and not able to implement reforms across all federal ministries.

The objective of ensuring that ample time is available to people working on the project (by allowing release from normal duties for a fixed period of time) has not been achieved, and most work has been done in addition to regular responsibilities. On the other hand, there has been considerable success in making information on the project available to a wide audience. A monthly **"information forum"** was established, and during 1990 and 1991 a regular series of meetings took place, to which were invited heads of departments in every ministry and other interested parties including representatives of staff unions and journalists. Between 200 and 400 people attended each of these briefing sessions. As a result, the initiatives were given big coverage in the monthly newsletter of the staff union which is circulated to some 200 000 staff.

The work of the in-depth analyses produced the following specific results:
- A report on the reduction of overlapping competences between departments was completed, and associated legislative initiatives are now planned for June 1992.
- Work on guidelines for information technology has been completed and the associated report is now ready for submission to the government for discussion.
- The group examining the use of buildings by the central federal administration completed its report in June 1991, and implementation of the proposals started in September under the responsibility of the Minister of Economic Affairs. A rather controversial part of this work is the notion that ministries should pay rent for the use of the buildings which they occupy, based on current market prices. An implication of this is that some ministries may relocate outside the city centre. Rents would be payable to the Ministry of Finance. The Ministry of Economic Affairs would, in turn, then arrange a contract with a privately-managed company to do building maintenance.
- The group which was set up to report on possible new telecommunication and computerisation systems finished its work, and as a result new regulations have been drafted which will be agreed by government in 1992. A pilot project has been set up; it deals with the "paperless office" (ELAC) and is being tested in the Ministry of Defence and part of the Federal Chancellery. In the future it is to examine paperless communication between ministries.

Financial management

The report on "Budgeting and Controlling" was largely finished in 1991 and implementation of its recommendations is expected to start in 1992. Two pilot projects are being developed. One will start in March 1992 and aims to evaluate the **efficiency** of personnel resources in the court system by assessing the numbers needed to run the system.

The second pilot project is in the Ministry of Public Economy and Transport and started at the end of 1991. It is examining the use of cost accounting as a means of improving **cost efficiency.** Procedures for permit applications are being analysed in five specific areas: the operation of cable cars; civil aviation; water police; trucking controls; and private car check-ups. The aim is to establish the best balance between administrative costs and charges to applicants. It is also intended to try to relate charges to the size of the proposed operation and its likely profits. After the accounting system has been examined, the next step will be to reduce the tasks and aims of ministries and then evaluate programme results.

Management of human resources

The inter-departmental study group on "Management and Personnel" finished its work and initiatives were launched relating to a number of its specific proposals. A **system of job descriptions** for the entire federal administration is being implemented by the responsible section of the Federal Chancellery and is expected to be completed for all ministries by February 1992. Similarly, the proposal to **decentralise personnel recruitment** has been implemented by introducing new legislation which shifts this responsibility to line ministries. The most controversial and discussed proposals relate to the **selection procedures for senior executive officers** in the administration. Whilst there is general agreement that the process can be improved, progress is proving difficult.

The **Federal Academy for Administration** (which is under the auspices of the Federal Chancellery) is responsible for implementing several proposals in the training field. One which gives emphasis to training in social and communication skills rather than professional training has already been included in the programme; and another aiming to improve on-the-job training for new entrants to the civil service is being developed with a view to implementation in 1992.

Some progress has also been made in the process of **co-determination** by the Federal Chancellery and the Ministry of Finance of human resource management across all federal ministries. This depends on law reform of the status of civil servants and is being discussed with representatives of the unions with a view to having new legislation by the end of 1992.

Two pilot projects are now being launched to test the **personnel development concept.** One, in the Ministry of Environment, Youth and Family, started at the end of 1991; the other, in the Ministry of Health, Sport and Consumer Protection, will begin in February 1992. Outside consultants have been contracted to help develop the pilot projects which should be completed during 1992. They aim to build up know-how for later application in all ministries.

Privatisation

Privatisation measures are one of the important issues in the "working programme" for the current legislative period of both parties in the present coalition government. The two parties have also agreed a list of fields in which privatisation should be initiated. Thus, according to a law passed in December 1991, the task of constructing dykes, for example, will in future be carried out by a private firm rather than the Ministry of Economic Affairs (which will however retain administrative powers concerning waterways). In some fields including civil aviation, private enterprise will also be entrusted with the exercise of administrative powers (issuing certain permits for airplanes, and directives for air traffic control).

The Austrian Railways, currently run by the State, are also to be privatised in the future. And a number of organisations in the fields of science, technology and research are also to be studied with a view to possible privatisation.

In Austria, civil servants working in bodies which are privatised can choose to either remain civil servants or to become private (contracted) employees of the enterprise. All staff appointed after privatisation are hired on a contract basis.

Organisational and structural change

The recent application by Austria for membership of the European Community has led to some fundamental discussions on the **relative roles of the Land and federal levels of government.** These are likely to continue for the next few years. In 1991 the Federal Chancellery took the initiative of establishing a study group composed of senior civil servants from both the federal and Land administrations and four university professors. The group examined the legal difficulties of the present distribution of responsibilities and made proposals. Political negotiations are expected to lead to an agreement within the next year on the main guidelines for reforming the distribution of responsibilities, after which preparations for a reform of the Constitution may begin.

FACTSHEET: AUSTRIA

A. PRINCIPAL RECENT PUBLIC MANAGEMENT DEVELOPMENTS

1988:
- Council of Ministers decides to launch Administrative Management Project (AMP) with aims including to:
  - tighten up the task and management structure;
  - increase productivity by 20 per cent over the next four years;
  - reduce cost of administrative activity;
  - concentrate on management tasks;
  - better balance the division of labour;
  - improve citizen-orientation of administration;
  - preserve departmental sovereignty.

1989:
- Implementation of AMP Phase One (preliminary analysis of problems) in 13 departments producing 3 696 proposals.

1990:
- AMP Phase Two (implementation of Phase One solutions and in-depth analysis).
- Implementation teams established in all departments under direction of project co-ordinator.
- Two interdepartmental in-depth study groups set up on "Management and Personnel" and "Budgeting and Controlling".

1991:
- The two study groups of the Administrative Management Project finish their work and submit their reports to the government.
- Four-member government team set up to fix implementation priorities and evaluate results of the project.
- Pilot projects set up in various ministries in the fields of cost accounting, personnel development, personnel efficiency, and the "paperless office".
- Study group set up to examine distribution of responsibilities between Federal and Land governments.

B. INSTITUTIONAL RESPONSIBILITY FOR PUBLIC MANAGEMENT IMPROVEMENT

ORGANISATION	TASKS AND RESPONSIBILITIES	OTHER INFORMATION
Federal Chancellery	– personnel policy across the federal administration – constitutional and legislative services and data protection issues – administrative reform – economic co-ordination and structural policies – IT policy and co-ordination – privatisation issues – co-ordination of auditing and control practices	The Federal Academy for Administration operates under the Federal Chancellery and is responsible for civil service training programmes.
Ministry of Finance	– budget process – improvement of financial management	

BELGIUM

The **Act of 21 March 1991** changed the status of certain public enterprises (Régie des Télégraphes et Téléphones-Belgacom; Régie des Postes-La Poste; Société Nationale des Chemins de Fer; Régie des Voies Aériennes). The aim of this Act was to:

- give freedom of management to the enterprises in question by concluding management contracts with them that specify their public service obligations and any funds to be provided by the State; and
- allow them to acquire stakes in private companies or to set up subsidiaries.

While affirming the public character of these enterprises, the Act endowed them with their own management structures and allowed them to bring in private capital. The enterprises remain subject to the law on procurement contracts. However, the Act, and particularly the provisions relating to the drawing up of management contracts, has still to be implemented.

The **Act of June 1991** on the restructuring of public credit institutions provided for a merger of the six existing institutions into two entities that would be better equipped to cope with competition and the harmonisation of the conditions of competition with private banks. It, too, has yet to come into force.

A **Royal Decree of 22 November 1991** was issued pursuant to the Act of 8 August 1988 which transferred powers to the Communities and Regions (including that of establishing the conditions of service of their personnel) with a view to ensuring that the Communities and Regions comply with certain common basic principles. The Royal Decree is intended, among other things, to:

- modernise the rules governing the rights and duties of staff, with emphasis on: loyalty (rather than obedience); responsiveness to users; communication (rather than the obligation on civil servants not to express their personal views in public); and the right to training;
- modernise the principle of appraisal with a view to making it a means of selecting staff for promotion, notably by introducing a quota system whereby civil servants with the highest ratings would automatically get priority for promotions;
- permit fixed-term appointments for some posts;
- create a new staff category for entrants to the civil service who have a short-cycle higher (non-university) education diploma; and
- enable staff to develop careers linked to the acquiring of a skill, while remaining in the same grade.

The **in-depth study of personnel requirements** continued in 1991. It covers the national "administrative" public service (80 000 people). The Public Service Counsellors of the A. B. C. Consultants Bureau, in the Ministry of the Interior and the Public Service, devised a methodology for drawing up organisation charts which involves:

- constructing organisation charts using the tools of systemic analysis and based on the concepts of:
  - products as quantifiable outcomes of activities aimed at outside users;
  - the classification of users;
  - product characteristics which allow the effectiveness of the products delivered to be appraised. These include volume, manpower costs, complexity, tolerances (difference between actual and desired time required to implement an activity), number of stages, nature, purpose, and use;

- characteristics of personnel such as age, rank, and skills (both existing and those that would be desirable, as determined by a classification of occupational skills established by the A. B. C. Consultants Bureau);
- writing the software for the input, checking and use of data; and
- setting up networks of:
  - executive heads (about 130) for whom the methodology is designed;
  - civil servants (about 300) whose task is to analyse data gathered from interviews with heads of service, and who have been trained in in-depth study concepts, interviewing techniques and software management.

In 1992 the A. B. C. Consultants Bureau will supplement this methodology with a programme of strategic thinking for executive heads. This will involve:

- playing a business game specially designed by the A. B. C. Consultants Bureau to acquaint executive heads with in-depth study concepts;
- discussing the role of general management or management bodies and the products needed, taking account of factors such as users' expectations, future events, strong and weak points, partners, competitors, etc.;
- analysing the existing situation in terms of: what is being done? how much is being done? how much does it cost in manpower? for whom is it being done? how long does it take? what skills are being used?; and
- planning steps (recruitment, training, computerisation, re-allocation of resources, information) to bring the existing situation in line with the desired objectives.

Under the **Act of 29 July 1991** requiring government departments to give reasons for administrative measures, users can demand to know the reasons for the decisions taken by departments (except in the cases provided for by the law).

Under a **co-operation agreement** with several Community and Regional executives, a committee was set up to propose ways of improving relations between government departments and users in areas where it was felt that co-ordination between executives could be improved.

An **agreement with the trade unions** has made possible a general overhaul of civil service pay scales. The aim of this overhaul, the final results of which are expected by 1994, is to match the pay for the various skills to labour market realities.

The **Information Technology Section** for the civil service was expanded with a view to developing an information technology policy for the public sector and providing advice on computerisation to those departments and agencies asking for it. The Section should be operational from 1992.

FACTSHEET: BELGIUM

A. PRINCIPAL RECENT PUBLIC MANAGEMENT DEVELOPMENTS

1985:   – Start of reform project to introduce programme budgets.

1986/87:   – Creation of the Secretariat for Modernisation and Computerisation of Public Agencies (attached to Prime Minister's Office).
    – Definition of a modernisation strategy implemented through a network of "modernisation units".

1988:   – Law of 8 August arranges for decentralisation of important powers from the central administration to the Communities and the Regions.
    – Decision of 7 October gives ministries and other public bodies a new method for managing recruitment using individual appropriations.
    – Twelve-point programme of action for IT introduced.

1989:   – Incentives provided by Government to set up "modernisation units" in ministries and other public bodies.
    – "College of Secretaries-General" established to advise the Minister of the Public Service.
    – Budgets presented by programme become part of the legal budget text, requiring approval by the legislature.

1990:   – Law of 15 January sets up a "clearing-house" bank for the social security administration.
    – Law of 20 February introduces single statute for civil servants.
    – LOGOS project launched to engage heads of administration in reforms.
    – Modernisation of selection techniques for recruitment.
    – Launch of in-depth study of personnel requirements.
    – "Master training plans" introduced as new management tool.
    – Role of Public Service Counsellors redefined by Royal Decree.

B. INSTITUTIONAL RESPONSIBILITY FOR PUBLIC MANAGEMENT IMPROVEMENT

ORGANISATION	TASKS AND RESPONSIBILITIES	OTHER INFORMATION
Ministry of the Interior and the Public Service – General Directorate for Selection and Training – General Administration Service – A.B.C. Consultants Bureau	– organisation, modernisation, and management of the public service; computerisation programme	Both the Minister of the Interior and the Minister of the Public Service have responsibility for the modernisation programme.
Cabinet of the Prime Minister	– managerial autonomy of public enterprises	
Ministry of Finance – Budget and Expenditure Control Division	– budgetary reform	
Cabinet of the Minister of the Budget	– budgetary reform	

CANADA

Significant progress has been achieved in 1991 in the process of renewal known as **Public Service 2000.** The reform of the Canadian Public Service hinges on four critical areas: service; people; innovation and empowerment; and accountability.

Service

The fundamental goal of Public Service 2000 is to **improve service** to Canada and to Canadians in an environment of increasingly scarce resources. Departments and agencies have started making improvements in service delivery by:

- developing, with the involvement of all staff in the organisation, **client-oriented mission statements;**
- examining existing **service standards** to see if they meet client expectations, and developing new ones. An *ad hoc* committee on service standards – composed of senior officials of line departments, the Treasury Board Secretariat, and the Office of the Comptroller General – was set up in the fall of 1991 to assist departments in this endeavour;
- adopting a new **consultative culture,** one that listens to clients, works in partnership with them, and adapts its operations to promote better service;
- **rating the quality** of services or identifying needed new ones through client surveys, toll-free lines, focus groups and panels;
- **delegating more authority** to the front-line staff; and
- increasing the use of **information technology.**

This emphasis on service will take time to be instilled throughout the Canadian Public Service. There is still a lot to do, in particular in the area of service standards.

People

Better people management is essential to better service. A number of measures were taken in 1991 to **streamline the structure** of the Public Service:

- A three-layer structure below the Deputy Minister was implemented across the Public Service.
- The first two levels of the Management Category were integrated, which resulted in a reduction from six classification levels to five.
- As a result of the 1991 Budget, the size of the Management Category is being reduced by 10 per cent from approximately 4 750 to 4 275 persons (it is expected that this reduction will be completed by 31 March 1993).
- The Management Category was renamed the Executive Group to recognise that it includes both managers and policy advisors.
- A task force was set up at the Treasury Board to develop a new simplified classification structure, which will be implemented by December 1993.

Several steps were taken in 1991 to make the Public Service more **people-oriented:**

- The first recruitment campaign for the **Management Trainee Programme** was successful in attracting 100 talented women and men from universities and 25 junior officers from within the Public Service. They will provide a pool of qualified middle managers from which senior executives of the future can be drawn.

- **Career assignment programmes** are being introduced in most departments to facilitate the movement of staff for career and organisational purposes.
- In November 1991, the Treasury Board adopted in principle the second report of the **Task Force on Staff Training and Development** which called for the creation of a "continuous learning culture". A special fund of C$ 10 million has also been set aside at the Treasury Board to support new departmental training initiatives.
- A new approach to setting **employment equity** targets was approved by the Treasury Board Secretariat in 1991. Targets are now based on rates of recruitment, promotion and separation, rather than on representation only. This reflects the principle that the workplace should be conducive to attracting and retaining designated group members (women, visible minorities, handicapped persons, and native people).
- **Progressive employment practices** – such as work-at-home, flexible hours, job-sharing, "upward feedback", and "bridging programmes" to help support staff enter the officer category – are being implemented across the Public Service.
- The **Human Resources Development Council** became the senior, official-level forum for implementing service-wide improvements in people management.

Innovation and empowerment

The Treasury Board Secretariat is well past the mid-point of bringing some major changes:

- **Operating budgets** were launched as pilots in 1991; full implementation is scheduled for April 1993.
- Greater **administrative authorities** with respect to purchasing, contracting, hospitality, etc., are being delegated to departments.
- A number of "**common services**" have become "optional"; departments can decide whether or not to use the services offered by the government.
- Nine new "**Special Operating Agencies**" were announced in 1991 in addition to the five already announced. As confidence grows, it is expected that further candidates for agency status will be identified.

Departments have also started to experiment with new initiatives – such as partnerships with labour and provincial governments in the area of training – to improve service to the public.

Accountability

In 1991, a new concept known as the "**Shared Management Agenda**" (SMA) was introduced by the Treasury Board and the Office of the Comptroller General. This is based on a more collaborative approach to the identification and resolution of larger management issues in the Public Service.

An SMA is essentially an agreement between the Deputy Minister of a department on the one hand, and the Secretary of the Treasury Board and the Comptroller General on the other, with respect to the major management issues at stake in that department – financial, human resources, information technology, etc. The SMA is intended to be simple, flexible, strategically oriented, and above all useful to departments, not a centrally-driven or paper-intensive exercise.

Legislation

In June 1991, the Government tabled legislation (Bill C-26) to amend the key pieces of Public Service employment legislation. This will provide the necessary legal foundation for:

- increased staffing efficiency while maintaining the merit principle as the basis of appointment and promotion in the Public Service;
- the establishment of employment equity programmes; and
- the simplification of collective bargaining.

Supplementary reference material

Public Service 2000 Task Force on Staff Training and Development. Second Report, May 1991.

FACTSHEET: CANADA

A. PRINCIPAL RECENT PUBLIC MANAGEMENT DEVELOPMENTS

1981: – Creation of a "Management Category" in the public service.

1984: – Specific Government focus on reducing public expenditure and increasing effectiveness and efficiency of public service operations.

1985: – Budget announces target of 15 000 person-years reduction over five years to 1990/91 and introduces possibility of privatising Crown corporations.

1986: – Increased Ministerial Authority and Accountability (IMAA) launched with aim of changing management culture of public service.
– Office of Privatisation and Regulatory Affairs set up.

1987: – Privatisation strategy adopted.

1988: – Creation of Canadian Centre for Management Development to promote teaching and training in public sector management.
– Memoranda of Understanding introduced as negotiated three-year agreement on accountability with performance indicators, expectations and targets.

1989: – Public Service 2000 initiative launched with aim of renewing the public service.
– New system of Cabinet decision-making announced.
– Personnel Management Manual streamlined.
– Administrative Policy Manual consolidated.
– Treasury Board Senior Advisory Committee re-established as inter-departmental consultative group.
– "Enterprising Management", a progress report on IMAA, issued.

1990: – Government White Paper on Public Service 2000 released reinforcing commitment to improving quality of service.
– Management Trainee Programme introduced to attract top graduates.
– Human Resources Development Council (HRDC) announced as a forum for senior Deputy Ministers, to provide strategic direction on human resource management.

1991: – Budget announces a wage freeze for 1991/92 and maximum increases of 3 per cent for the following two years; a 10 per cent reduction in the Management Category; a freeze in capital spending and non-wage operating budgets; and a freeze in the performance pay of members of the Management Category.
– Functions of the Office of Privatisation and Regulatory Affairs redeployed to the Department of Finance.

B. INSTITUTIONAL RESPONSIBILITY FOR PUBLIC MANAGEMENT IMPROVEMENT

ORGANISATION	TASKS AND RESPONSIBILITIES	OTHER INFORMATION
Privy Council Office (PCO)	– support and advice to the Prime Minister and Cabinet on organisational and legislative changes for the public service – management of the Public Service 2000 initiative	
Public Service Commission (PSC)	– application of merit in staffing; recruitment to, promotion within and staffing of the Management Category	Independent agency, accountable to Parliament.
Treasury Board Secretariat (TBS)	– general management of financial, human and material resources, concerning both policy and expenditure proposals – management of the IMAA process – management of the ''Shared Management Agenda'' process	
Canadian Centre for Management Development	– research and training for managerial modernisation	
Department of Finance	– management of regulatory process, under the responsibility of the Minister of State (Finance and Privatisation).	

DENMARK

In May 1991, the Danish Government submitted a report on the Danish Modernisation Programme 1991 to Parliament. The Programme states that the public sector of the 1990s will be characterised by:

- a development which **places the citizens in the centre** with better and cheaper solutions enabling a lower burden of taxation; and
- intensified **internationalisation** and increased interaction with the European Community.

Based on the marked developments of the public sector in the 1980s, a new pattern – "a change of system" – of problem-solving and management mechanisms is expected to emerge in the 1990s. The main features of this new pattern are:

- a market-type model for production of public services;
- public tasks carried out in the best and cheapest way, whether the production be public or private;
- increased demands on results and more independence for public institutions;
- relaxation of rules and regulations;
- result-oriented personnel policies with more liberty of action for professional efforts; and
- new types and structures of organisation in the State, counties and municipalities.

In 1991, the following concrete steps were taken.

Organisational and structural change

Elements of a **market-type model** are being introduced in several public service areas. The main elements are: a greater freedom of choice for citizens (users); block appropriations following the users (through taximetre systems); and competition between more independent institutions, with management normally responsible to an independent board. In 1991, this model was implemented in its most complete form at polytechnics and business schools. The Government has set out reform proposals along similar lines in the following areas: nurseries and kindergartens; and hospitals, where a new health bill will enable citizens to choose more freely between hospitals.

Contracting out is another example of the use of market-type mechanisms in the public sector. Based on the work and recommendations carried out by a committee in 1991, new rules to promote contracting out will come into effect in 1992.

In 1991, new **privatisations** also took place. These concerned Giro-Bank, Tele-Danmark (telecommunications), and Datacentralen (computer services). In 1992, a minority of shares will be sold in the private sector.

On the basis of a pilot study completed in May 1991, seven experiments with **"free agencies"** will be carried out from 1st January 1992. The selected State agencies and institutions will be given more managerial freedom, among other things, in the areas of appropriation and staff. In return, demands for results will be increased.

Better quality service delivery and client satisfaction

In order to improve services to citizens, companies, municipalities, etc., the Government has initiated new projects on service and quality in ministries, government agencies, etc. Specific criteria of success are defined for each of these projects. The Ministry of Finance has published a guide on criteria of success and measuring results.

Financial management

Agreements on budget frameworks for a four-year period are an important element in the contracts for several "free agencies" mentioned above. This will provide more stable frameworks for re-organisation initiatives of the areas in question.

Management of human resources

As part of the 1991 collective agreements, the system of local and individual wage supplements in the public sector has been further developed. A new agreement has also been reached on the distribution of a part of rationalisation and efficiency surpluses to personnel in agencies which take part in "free agency" experiments.

Supplementary reference material

Ministry of Finance. *The Public Sector in the Year 2000. Report on the Danish Modernization Programme 1991.* Department of Management and Personnel, Copenhagen, May 1991 (ISBN 87-503-9182-8).

FACTSHEET: DENMARK

A. PRINCIPAL RECENT PUBLIC MANAGEMENT DEVELOPMENTS

1983:   –   Modernisation Programme for the Public Sector introduced with aims of increasing efficiency and improving service quality at all levels of administration and improving motivation and job satisfaction.

1983-85:   –   First Phase of Modernisation Programme offers incentives for modernisation including relaxed control on expenditure and number of posts in each ministry.
–   Information and publicity campaign for Programme launched.
–   Deregulation programme started.

1986/87:   –   Second Phase of Modernisation Programme: each ministry prepares implementation plans with sectoral goals according to Ministry of Finance guidelines.
–   Scheme for compulsory rotation of professional staff introduced.

1988/89:   –   Third Phase of Modernisation Programme with comprehensive "Review of the Public Sector 1988" produced by Ministry of Finance increasing emphasis on reducing public expenditure.
–   Similar review in 1989 includes focus on reducing personnel and further decentralisation.
–   Debureaucratisation initiative launched with aim of reducing, simplifying, and decentralising administrative functions and improving citizen orientation.

1990:   –   Government submits evaluation of Modernisation Programme to Parliament.
–   Major technical reform of central government budgeting and appropriation system (to take effect in 1991) includes a more programme-oriented structure and modernisation of the computerised system.
–   Government policy for management development in the 1990s.

1991:   –   Government submits the programme "The Public Sector in the Year 2000" to Parliament.
–   Experiments with "free agencies".
–   Projects on service and quality within all ministerial areas.

B. INSTITUTIONAL RESPONSIBILITY FOR PUBLIC MANAGEMENT IMPROVEMENT

ORGANISATION	TASKS AND RESPONSIBILITIES	OTHER INFORMATION
Ministry of Finance		
– Department of Management and Personnel	– personnel and administrative policy; co-ordination of public sector modernisation programme	
– Department of the Budget	– budgeting and expenditure control	
Prime Minister's Office	– co-ordination of the debureaucratisation initiative	A council of ministers co-ordinates the debureaucratisation initiative with the assistance of a committee of permanent secretaries which is chaired by the Prime Minister's Office.

FINLAND

Policy context, goals and priorities

The present Government came into office in May 1991. One of the main economic policy objectives of the Government is to restrict the growth of public expenditure. Public management reform has been specified as one of the Government's priorities. According to its programme, the Government's objective is to develop administrative structures that guarantee flexible, effective and fair service delivery without expanding the public sector.

Improved quality of public services is the overall objective. The Government has set as its public management priorities: effectiveness, productivity, decentralisation, and the reform of central government guidance. The present Government has set up (as did its predecessor) a permanent Ministerial Committee to guide and monitor the reform process and to introduce new initiatives.

The public management improvement functions of the Ministry of Finance were re-organised in 1991. The Public Management Department of the Ministry is now organised according to result-targeted projects instead of the standard office structure.

Organisational and structural change, and decentralisation

In October 1991, the Government launched a major project on **decentralisation** and reform of central government organisations. The project builds on the work previously initiated by the Decentralisation Committee in 1986 and on the ongoing reform of public enterprises. The new project aims at giving new impetus to rationalising decentralisation efforts. The project is carried out under a Project Leader assisted by a secretariat.

One new **public enterprise** started operation in 1991, when the National Civil Aviation Organisation was transformed into a public enterprise.

Some central government **re-organisations** took place in 1991. The National Board of Social Affairs and the National Board of Health were merged into one central agency called the Central Agency for Social Affairs and Health. Similarly, the National Board of General Education and the National Board of Vocational Education were merged into the Central Agency for Education.

The **managerial structure** of central agencies has been under revision: there now remain only a couple of central agencies with the old type of collegia as the highest decision-making bodies. The rest of the central agencies now have managerial boards.

In December 1991, the Government presented to Parliament a proposal on legislative reform of **State aid** to municipalities, which will come into force from the beginning of 1993. The rationale of this reform is to increase the self-government and economic responsibility of the municipalities. The objective is to improve the economy and effectiveness of the municipalities and to change the accounting basis of State aid from a sectorally expenditure-based system to one based on the socio-economic conditions of the municipalities. The new system will give the municipalities more scope to organise their own activities and administrations.

Management of policy-making

The **delegation of tasks** from the general session of the Cabinet to the ministries, which began in 1987, has resulted in reducing the number of Cabinet decisions by 840 per year between 1987 and 1990. A new legislative proposal, which codifies the delegation of tasks from the Cabinet to the ministries and also within the ministries, is planned for presentation to Parliament at the beginning of 1992.

A new project, started in 1991, aims to develop a common information processing system for decision-making in the different ministries.

Better quality service delivery and client satisfaction

Since 1989, the Ministry of Finance has conducted a **Service Project** with the aim of improving the quality of public service delivery. Within this framework, a "Good Service Office" competition was organised in 1990. Experiments with one-stop shops have been carried out and a significant amount of supporting material for public agencies has been produced. The editing of a *Citizen's Service Guidebook* is under way, and it is to be published in 1992.

The information technology function of the Ministry of Finance has been re-organised. The trend is towards overall guidance and co-ordination instead of detailed central decision-making. The focus in the IT field is on building up a technology network throughout the public administration.

Financial management

In February 1991, the Government gave politically-binding budgetary ceilings to ministries for 1992 and the two following years. They were reconfirmed by the new post-election Cabinet at the end of April 1991.

Budget proposals include a more result-oriented budget structure for 12 major agencies in the 1991 budget, and for 30 other agencies in the 1992 proposal. The new approach will be extended to all agencies in the 1995 budget. In connection with the 1992 budget proposal, the number of expenditure items is a little more than one thousand. The reform of public enterprises will continue.

The development project team on result-oriented budgeting submitted its final report to the Ministry of Finance in June 1991. The project team prepared many study reports on different subjects.

In May 1991, the Government presented to Parliament an **economic policy statement** in which the basic problem is identified as the fact that both the internal and the external balance of the Finnish economy have been shaken. The Government intends that the annual real growth rate of central government expenditure must be zero per cent to the year 1995, and 1-2 per cent in the whole public sector.

The Government has decided to strengthen the infrastructure for the use of **market mechanisms.** There are three simultaneous government-wide development processes going on in this field:

- unbiasing the cost attribution (personnel costs such as pensions, office space and other premises of the agencies, asset management including the cost of capital, internal pricing of services);
- strengthening accounting systems to support the result-oriented approach to budgeting and management; and
- increasing managerial freedom and incentives (*ex ante* financial controls have been mostly removed and replaced by agreements between the ministry and the agencies on the results to be achieved).

There have been some major legislative developments in budgeting, such as the implementation of an amendment to the Constitution concerning state finances, changes in the budget law (net budgeting), and a new law on user charges. Parliament passed the amendment to the Constitution in summer 1991, and both law bills were given to Parliament during the autumn 1991 session.

Management of human resources

A policy decision was made by the Government in March 1991 concerning the development of government personnel policy and personnel management. The decision is aimed to direct development during 1991-95. According to the decision, which results from proposals submitted by the **Personnel Committee** in 1990, personnel policy should become more flexible, competitive, active, decentralised, and streamlined, to meet the demands of the late 1990s. Specific projects to be undertaken are as follows:

- reform of the legal status of civil servants;
- reform of the terms of the employment relationship and pay;
- improvement of personnel training and development;
- improvement of management resources and development;
- improvement of recruitment;
- promotion of better working teams, co-operation and leadership;
- promotion of equality between the sexes;
- decentralisation of personnel management and modernisation of the procedures.

The Ministry of Finance set up a **task force on the reform of legal status and employment** in May 1991, to prepare concrete proposals for new legislation by the end of 1992. Instead of two kinds of government employee (civil servants according to civil service legislation, and employees according to general labour legislation), a **uniform employment category** will be developed corresponding as much as possible to the general labour legislation. A consensus with the unions has been achieved on the general objectives of the reform. A similar project has also been started with municipalities.

Consequently, the systems of **collective bargaining** and **agreements** are to be unified by the same task force, following the practices used in the private labour market. A more decentralised system is needed, giving more discretionary powers to make agreements at the agency level. A number of measures to decentralise bargaining have already been taken, for example negotiations concerning merit pay and productivity bonuses.

Reform of the **terms of the employment relationship and pay** has been continued, including experiments with basic pay based on a new classification of jobs according to qualifications (a survey covering all personnel has been done), merit pay and productivity bonuses. About 10 per cent of the personnel is covered by the merit pay and productivity bonus schemes. A uniform general framework and core criteria are given centrally, but the applications are made in each agency. Consensus with the unions is presumed. In most cases, experiments are conducted in agencies which also have the new result-oriented budgeting system. Recent follow-up surveys and evaluations report mainly positive effects.

In December 1991, the **Pensions Committee** submitted its proposals for the reform of pension systems. These include a proposal to harmonise the pensions of civil servants along the lines used in the private sector. This means in practice raising the retirement age from 63 to 65, cutting the level of benefits, and lengthening the service period necessary to qualify for a full pension.

Reduction of personnel numbers has continued, based on the Government decisions of 1989 and 1990. In 1989 it was decided that a cut of 2 800 had to be made during 1990/91; and the 1990 decision required that 10 per cent of vacancies coming open in 1991 be left unfilled. A new decision was made by the Government in 1991 as a part of the budget for 1992 and the financial frames for 1992-95. The recent objective is, in addition to the previous cuts, to reduce the number of posts in state administration by 5 per cent in 1992-95, from about 130 000 to 123 500 (excluding public enterprises). Each ministry is preparing to implement the cuts, mainly based on voluntary mobility and retirement.

Reduction procedures are combined with budgetary reform so that cuts in personnel are also automatically made in the annual financial frames of each ministerial branch. The frames of personnel numbers are also decided by the Government in the budget for each branch for the next five years. Public enterprises are excluded, though they have nevertheless prepared plans for reducing the total number of their personnel (approximately 83 000) by several thousands in 1992-95 to improve their profitability and ability to compete.

A special project will be set up in January 1992 to improve **personnel training.** The increasing average age of personnel – as well as rapid changes in organisations, duties and technology – requires improvements in training. More retraining is also needed to avoid giving notice, to redeploy and relocate personnel, and to increase flexibility. The Government also decided in 1991 to decrease considerably the number of **formal qualifications** for civil service posts created by law or act. The qualifications still considered necessary (for example, university degrees) will be reformulated more broadly and flexibly. The aim is to improve recruitment and facilitate restructuring of organisations and duties.

A special **management training programme** was started in September 1991 for approximately 100 top civil servants (permanent secretaries, general directors, etc.). The aims of this ''Development Programme for National Strategy'' are: to support and increase the commitment of top civil servants to the changes needed in the public sector; to improve the ability of the national strategy to adjust to national and international changes; and to improve strategic management, management of change, and leadership.

A new kind of **co-operation and cross-fertilisation between the private and public sectors** is being attempted in this training programme. In each group of approximately 25 persons there are on average five top managers from the private sector. The participants are invited by the Prime Minister. The programme is executed by a private-sector management training institute. Within the next four years, the whole target group will have undertaken this three-week training exercise. Another programme for the next managerial level (approximately 400 participants) has been planned and will start in autumn 1992, to be executed by the Administrative Development Agency. These two programmes represent the corporate-level management training of State government. Other measures to develop management resources (recruitment, appointment, assessment, career, mobility, etc.) will be started in early 1992.

Regulatory review and reform

By the end of 1990, all government agencies were obliged to renew their regulations. Some 1 800 regulations have been abolished, but 6 500 regulations are still in force. Public agencies are now obliged by law to keep a register of their regulations. The register became publicly available at the beginning of 1992.

Within the project conducted by the Ministry of Finance on the reform of licencing systems, some 70 requirements for licences have been abolished. Further work is needed, since the total number of licence requirements is still about 2 000. Current work focuses particularly on licences concerning enterprises and competition. Some fields are treated in slightly different ways than others. In the field of environmental protection, for example, the objective is to rationalise the administrative system (for example by merging several licence requirements) rather than abolish requirements.

Monitoring and evaluation

One of the roles of the permanent Ministerial Committee is to monitor the reform process of public management. For this purpose, the Public Management Department of the Ministry of Finance prepares follow-up material. A specific follow-up exercise is planned to evaluate the results of the Service Project mentioned above.

FACTSHEET: FINLAND

A. PRINCIPAL RECENT PUBLIC MANAGEMENT DEVELOPMENTS

1986:
- Proposals by Parliamentary Committee to decentralise decision-making.
- Government decision outlining regulatory reform.

1987:
- Permanent Ministerial Committee established to guide and monitor reform measures throughout the administration.
- Administrative Development Agency set up to promote reform in agencies by providing training and consultancy services.

1988:
- Approval of first programme for implementing reforms.
- "Service Declaration" defines general principles for improving public service delivery.
- General legislation on public enterprises comes into force.
- Government guidelines set on decentralising decision-making.
- New decree on use of information technology in central government.

1989:
- Approval of second programme for implementing reforms.
- Government decision to reduce number of posts in administration by 1.3 per cent by end of 1991.
- First new types of public enterprises start operation.
- Proposal to re-organise management of central agencies (National Boards).
- Start of Free Municipality Experiment in 56 municipalities.
- Ministry of Finance decides new instructions to reform State Budget implementation procedures.
- Launch of research project by Ministry of Finance on measuring productivity in public sector.
- Three-year project initiated by Ministry of Communications to develop a national information and services network.
- Committee set up to make proposals on a productivity-based bonus system, a more individualised pay system, and more decentralised authority to restructure the classification of posts.
- Reform started to simplify procedures for permits and licences.
- Government White Paper on information management in central government and the role of IT in administrative reform.

1990:
- Government report on reform of public administration transmitted to Parliament for discussion.
- Budget proposals include more result-oriented budget structure for three major agencies (and for 12 others in the 1991 proposals).
- New Act requires central agencies to renew their ordinances and regulations by end of 1990.
- State Railways and Post and Telecommunications start to operate as new types of public enterprises.
- Personnel Committee submits proposals to reform personnel policy.
- Government decision to leave unfilled 10 per cent of posts coming open in 1991.

B.   INSTITUTIONAL RESPONSIBILITY FOR PUBLIC MANAGEMENT IMPROVEMENT

ORGANISATION	TASKS AND RESPONSIBILITIES	OTHER INFORMATION
Ministry of Finance – Public Management Department	– improvement of the delivery of public services, managerial capacities, administrative procedures and regulatory system	Provides secretarial assistance to the permanent Ministerial Committee which guides and follows up public management improvement.
– Personnel Department	– personnel policies and human resources management – reform of the terms of the employment relationship and pay – personnel volume management – guidelines of personnel development and training – guidelines of management development and training	
– Budget Department	– budgetary reform, financial management, and productivity and efficiency measurement	
Administrative Development Agency (ADA)	– consultancy support for managerial improvement and in-service training for government agencies	Autonomous agency under the Ministry of Finance.
Ministry of the Interior	– issues related to regional and local administration – decentralisation; strengthening municipal autonomy	
Prime Minister's Office	– development of Cabinet decision-making procedures	

FRANCE

Organisational and structural change

A law on regional and local administration was enacted on 6 February 1992. It aims to redefine the role of the central civil service and of regional and local administration, and to propose new forms of co-operation between regional and local authorities (especially municipalities).

This law reverses the division of responsibilities between the central administration and decentralised bodies of the State; henceforth, the latter have powers under common law, while the central administration only has exceptional powers. This law – which will soon be followed by a "decentralisation charter" – has already prompted government agencies to consider their future re-organisation into "poles of competence" around the prefects, so as better to meet the needs of regional and local authorities. Experiments are currently under way in the Ministries of Agriculture, Public Facilities, Social Affairs, and Environment. Government agencies are redefining their tasks with a view to improving planning and evaluation.

Lastly, the transformation of the Posts and Telecommunications (PTT) into two public establishments was completed during 1991, resulting in the introduction of new management methods. Now, the Post and France Télécom are two independent establishments linked to the State by planning contracts.

Management of policy-making

The trend towards devolving decision-making as much as possible continued. Thus, 101 measures designed to decentralise regulatory procedures, which were decided at the end of December 1990, are now being implemented. They relate to all areas of government activity, and aim to make local actors more accountable. Before implementing these measures, however, the government considered that it was first necessary to consult closely with all the partners concerned – trade unions, public servants, users. This is gradually being done.

Better quality service delivery and client satisfaction

This is one of the main thrusts of the policy of "**renewal of the public service**" which was launched in 1988, and one of the key items on the agenda of the government seminar held on 11 April 1991, which brought together under the Prime Minister all the members of the government. Following the introduction of this policy, there are now 470 "service projects" and 85 centres of accountability in government agencies, the aim of which is to provide a better service to the public.

User committees have been set up at local and regional level (to represent users *vis-à-vis* the PTT or the Ministry of Finance). The simplification of administrative formalities is being encouraged and developed at both the regional and the national level (Commission for the Simplification of Administrative Formalities of Businesses, COSIFORME). To improve user information, data banks that can be accessed on a decentralised basis are being set up. Lastly, each government department is drawing up "golden rules" for the public service, which set out the rights and obligations of both users and the administration.

A "**Public Service Charter**" is being developed. Its aims are to define the new guiding principles to serve as the foundation for the public service in France; to enable measurement of the success of actions undertaken by the central administration; to enable public agencies to place the user at the centre of their preoccupations; and to define objectives for obtaining a better public service, as set by ministers. This Charter will be adopted by the Council of Ministers, will be revised each year, and will be the subject of a report to Parliament.

Financial management

The government seminar held on 11 April 1991 spawned numerous measures designed to simplify budgetary and accounting procedures (appropriations to be less specific, introduction of *ex post* auditing, improvements to imprest and revenue accounts).

The number of "centres of accountability" has now increased to 85, and an assessment of their first year of operation is now under way. This assessment will probably show that more managerial flexibility is required, i.e. that the steps taken to increase operational flexibility do not go far enough, and that greater collective and individual accountability for the services provided is needed.

Management of human resources

The seminar held on 11 April 1991 decided that civil service competitions for **recruitment** should be modernised with a view to making them more vocationally-oriented. The trade unions will be consulted on the changes, which will be submitted to the Conseil économique et social for an opinion.

To ensure that **training** is tailored as closely as possible to needs, interministerial block appropriations for training will be decentralised to the regional prefects. Six-month training courses will be organised for executive heads by the Directorate General for Administration and the Public Service, and each ministry.

Under the Act of 26 July 1991, nationals of member countries of the **European Community** will henceforth be eligible for public employment in France. Furthermore, the secondment of French public servants to other countries in Europe is being encouraged, and a European training programme for 2 000 senior civil servants is being implemented.

Monitoring and evaluation

On 21 March 1991, the Comité interministériel de l'évaluation (Interministerial Committee on Evaluation) selected five areas of public policy for evaluation: rehabilitation of public housing; social integration of young people with problems; reception of underprivileged sections of the community by public services; children's school and leisure hours; and the impact of the expansion of information technology on administrative efficiency. The appraisal of this last area was due to be completed by the end of December 1991. Five new areas of public policy are also being considered for evaluation; one of them – government social policy – has already been approved by the Conseil scientifique de l'évaluation (Scientific Committee on Evaluation).

FACTSHEET: FRANCE

A. PRINCIPAL RECENT PUBLIC MANAGEMENT DEVELOPMENTS

1982/83:
- Decentralisation Acts modify division of responsibilities between local authorities and central government.
- Economic restructuring includes dual aims of salary constraint and staff reductions in the public service.

1988:
- Pay agreement signed with five of seven public servant trade unions.
- Two decrees increase possibilities of promotion by widening number of candidates for selection and guaranteeing a minimum proportion of automatic appointments.
- Reform of administrative courts started.

1989:
- Prime Ministerial circular and seminar on "Renewal of the Public Service" expresses new concepts and priorities concerning public management, i.e. more dynamic personnel management and more effectiveness by increasing managerial responsibilities in ministries and agencies.
- Framework Agreement on continuing training signed with five unions.
- Publication and discussion of report on modernisation of the public administration by Economic and Social Council.
- Work by committee on government effectiveness for preparation of Tenth Plan.
- Every ministry required to submit a "modernisation plan", including an IT master plan by end of summer.
- Several Government reforms launched concerning decentralisation, work organisation and administrative simplification.

1990:
- Second government seminar led by Prime Minister to define, evaluate and accelerate implementation of management reform measures.
- Protocol of Agreement signed with five public servant trade unions specifying changes to qualifications and salary scales.
- Over 200 "service projects" adopted to redefine responsibilities between different levels of the State administration.
- 60 "centres of accountability" set up to allow more flexible management.
- Diagnosis of decentralised State administration in each region.
- 29 regional colloquia and a national meeting aim at heightening awareness of public service renewal efforts.
- Interministerial Committee on Evaluation set up with own budget and chaired by Prime Minister or his representative.
- "Innovation network" set up by Directorate General for Administration and the Public Service aimed at promoting practical modernisation measures.
- 180 decentralisation and regulatory simplification measures identified.
- Reform of Post and Telecommunication services starts.

1991:
- Third government seminar on the renewal of the public service noted progress so far and the continuation of measures begun in 1989.
- Salary agreement signed with four public servant trade unions, for fixing global evolution of pay through February 1993.
- Commission for the Renewal of the Public Service set up to consider the major modernisation themes. Members include representatives from public servant trade unions and from the administration, and experts; it is chaired by the Minister for the Public Service.

B. INSTITUTIONAL RESPONSIBILITY FOR PUBLIC MANAGEMENT IMPROVEMENT

ORGANISATION	TASKS AND RESPONSIBILITIES	OTHER INFORMATION
Ministry for the Public Service and Administrative Modernisation – Directorate General for Administration and the Public Service	– inter-ministerial co-ordination of management of public personnel	
Council of State	– advice to the government on legal and administrative issues; reform proposals; final court of appeal in administrative matters	
General Secretariat of the Government	– organisation of the government's work	Directly linked to the Prime Minister.
Interministerial Committee for Information Technology and Office Automation in Government (CIIBA)	– define policies for the use of IT in government agencies; training of public servants	Under the authority of the Prime Minister and the General Secretariat of the Government.
Ministry of Economy, Finance and the Budget – Budget Directorate	– management and reform of budgetary, accounting and financial procedures in all ministries	
General Planning Commission	– draw up and implement national plans for medium and long term	Under the authority of the Prime Minister.
Court of Auditors	– supervision of the use of government funds and the implementation of financial legislation	A Central Committee of Enquiry examines the costs and productivity of public service delivery.

GERMANY

Seat of the Federal Government

The Unification Treaty, which established German unity, proclaimed the city of Berlin as the capital of Germany, but left it up to a later decision whether the federal constitutional organs should take their seat in Berlin or Bonn. On 20 June 1991, after a controversial debate, the Federal Parliament (Bundestag) decided that the seat of the Bundestag would be Berlin. This decision includes the expectation that the Federal Government will move the core spheres of governmental functions to Berlin.

On 11 December 1991, the Federal Government decided upon the distribution of the federal governmental authorities between Berlin and Bonn: of the current 18 federal ministries, 10 shall move to Berlin and 8 shall stay in Bonn. The following federal ministries and authorities are expected to take their seat in Berlin:

- Federal Chancellery;
- Federal Press Office;
- Federal Foreign Office;
- Federal Ministry of the Interior;
- Federal Ministry of Justice;
- Federal Ministry of Finance;
- Federal Ministry of Economics;
- Federal Ministry of Labour and Social Affairs;
- Federal Ministry for the Family;
- Federal Ministry of Transport;
- Federal Ministry for Women and Youth;
- Federal Ministry for Regional Planning, Building and Urban Development.

The decision of the Federal Government does not include a time schedule, but it is expected that within a period of ten to twelve years the removal will be completed.

The federal ministries which will stay in Bonn are:

- Federal Ministry of Food, Agriculture and Forests;
- Federal Ministry of Defence;
- Federal Ministry for Health;
- Federal Ministry for Environmental Protection;
- Federal Ministry for Research and Technology;
- Federal Ministry of Posts and Telecommunications;
- Federal Ministry for Economic Co-operation;
- Federal Ministry of Education and Science.

Certain directorates of those federal ministries moving to Berlin will, however, keep their seat in Bonn. Therefore, of 21 200 places of employment in the federal ministries, 13 900 (or 65 per cent) will remain in Bonn.

Administrative development in the five eastern Länder

The setting up of state and local administrations in the five eastern Länder is still proceeding. The Federal Government and the western Länder provide for substantial financial and personnel aid.

Administrative aid is co-ordinated by a **joint clearing office** which has its secretariat within the Federal Ministry of the Interior.

In the eastern Länder, the great lack of qualified administrative staff is not yet resolved. To attract experienced civil servants to work on the basis of limited-time secondment in eastern Germany, **special financial allowances** have been created. More than 20 000 civil servants of the Federation, western Länder and local governments now work in eastern Germany.

Large-scale **training** and qualification measures are being carried out to equip the staff of the former east German administration with the know-how to work in the public administration of a constitutional state. The Federal Academy of Public Administration offers a wide range of seminars to the personnel of the eastern Länder and local administrations as part of the Federal Training Assistance Programme. With regard to the **re-organisation of local government,** the Federal Ministry of the Interior provides financial support for training programmes, projects on the organisational development of local self-government, and personnel expenses.

FACTSHEET: GERMANY

A. PRINCIPAL RECENT PUBLIC MANAGEMENT DEVELOPMENTS

1983: – Government resolution to promote debureaucratisation and simplification of law and administration and to set up an Independent Commission within the Federal Ministry of the Interior.

1983-86: – Improved flexibility in working time, especially concerning part-time jobs.

1986-89: – Amendment to Federal Budget Code to create a uniform accounting system in three steps involving organisational simplification and better use of IT.

1988: – Federal Cabinet defines "Guidelines for the use of IT in the Federal Administration".

1989: – Federal Ministers of Interior and Justice present strategy to Cabinet for improving federal legislation.

1990: – Unification Treaty ends division of the two German States and makes provision for transitional arrangements for administrative institutions, legal status of personnel and financial management in eastern Germany.
– Federal Academy of Public Administration embarks on major in-service training programme for the new Länder.

1991: – Federal Parliament (Bundestag) decides that the seat of Parliament and the Federal Government will be Berlin. The removal from Bonn to Berlin will take place within the next ten years. However, a number of federal ministries and authorities will remain in Bonn.

B. INSTITUTIONAL RESPONSIBILITY FOR PUBLIC MANAGEMENT IMPROVEMENT

ORGANISATION	TASKS AND RESPONSIBILITIES	OTHER INFORMATION
Federal Ministry of the Interior – General Directorate 'D' (public service law) – General Directorate 'O' (organisation)	– general responsibility limited to matters relating to the public service and to public service law, including IT and training	Improvement of public management is decentralised to the federal states. Every Minister has independent competence for his sector within guidelines set by the Chancellor.
Independent Federal Commission to Simplify Law and Administration	– promotion of debureaucratisation and deregulation; streamlining of administrative procedures	Appointed by Cabinet; within the Federal Ministry of the Interior.
Federal Academy of Public Administration	– in-service training; research on public administration and public management reform	Under the authority of the Federal Ministry of the Interior.
Federal Chancellery	– general co-ordination and setting of guidelines	
Federal Ministry of Finance	– budget process	

GREECE

The law on "Modernisation of the Organisation and Functioning of the Public Administration and the Upgrading of Public Personnel" was enacted in 1991. It consolidates the recent attempts to modernise public administration in Greece. The main elements of this law are described below.

Organisational modernisation

The **public sector is redefined,** including a restructuring of legal entities under public law and rationalisation of their functioning. Attempts have already been made to reduce the size of the public sector through legislative intervention, in order to release a number of legal entities under private law from legal obligations and bureaucratic procedures which are considered unsuitable to their nature and scope.

Functional modernisation

In the field of **service delivery** improvements:
- Deadlines have been established for the delivery of services. If deadlines are not met, an indemnity must be paid to the citizen.
- Simplification of procedures and a shortening of the time for issuing administrative documents are being sought by delegating authority for signature and reducing powers.
- A committee has been established to compile a "Code on the Relations between the Public Administration and the Citizen".

A system has been established for maintaining a regularly updated description of the responsibilities and duties of every unit in the central administration. This information has already been gathered in the Ministry to the Presidency of Government, and its elaboration will start soon.

Regulatory review and reform

A committee has been established for the simplification of legislation and of other administrative acts. The main purpose is to restrict multiple legislation and unnecessary bureaucratic procedures.

Human resource management

A **new system of recruitment** in the public sector has been established. Recruitments will in future be based on anticipated needs and will be filled by means of an annual nation-wide competition. A central committee – independent of government – will guarantee the impartiality and fairness of the competition. However, this competition did not take place in 1991, as a result of the Government's decision to suspend recruitment in the public sector (a decision taken in the framework of government policy for a reduction in public expenditure and in the number of public employees).

A more rational allocation of personnel in the different parts of the public sector and a more rational use of human resources are to be pursued by means of transfers (the principle of **mobility**).

A comprehensive system for **continuing education and training** of personnel is to be put in place by the following measures:

– the introduction of compulsory training for personnel during their careers by setting up various categories of training programmes (introductory education for new entrants during their two-year probationary period, training, specialisation, advanced training, further education, and post-graduate studies);
– the establishment of new training units in public services and in legal entities under public law;
– setting up a network of pilot units for on-the-job training of personnel; and
– inter-relating education with career development and promotion.

A special committee for the compilation of a new "Code for the Public Service" has been established.

A new system of **employee evaluation** will be introduced. The system has been designed in such a way as to guarantee an objective and reliable evaluation of professional capacity and adequacy. A Presidential Decree on this is soon to be put into force.

A system of bonuses and awards (pecuniary and non-pecuniary) for employees who have performed their duties exceptionally well is being institutionalised.

FACTSHEET: GREECE

A. PRINCIPAL RECENT PUBLIC MANAGEMENT DEVELOPMENTS

1982: – Introduction of government policy to improve citizen-administration relations.

1983-89: – Extensive devolution of powers from central to prefectural government along with strengthening of role and powers of local government and associated improvements in financial management.

1985: – Legislation to reform regulatory framework for citizen-administration relations including simplification of procedures and strengthening of citizens' rights.

1988: – 13 new regional planning authorities established under central government control but with local representation.

1989: – New government's programme includes emphasis on tighter control of government expenditure and stabilisation of public sector employment.
– Ministerial committee established to control recruitment to the civil service and the public sector in general.
– A circular from the Minister to the Presidency of Government introduces an embargo on recruitment in the public sector.
– Committee set up at the initiative of Ministry to the Presidency of Government to study launching of administration-wide public management reforms.

1990: – New legislation redefines and reduces public sector to a "more effective" area.
– Major programme of privatisation of "problematic" public enterprises.
– General-directorates established to improve co-ordination of services.
– Units of strategic planning analysis and of policy evaluation established.
– Participation in training, re-education or specialisation programmes defined as obligatory for public service career development.

B. INSTITUTIONAL RESPONSIBILITY FOR PUBLIC MANAGEMENT IMPROVEMENT

ORGANISATION	TASKS AND RESPONSIBILITIES	OTHER INFORMATION
Ministry to the Presidency of Government	– overall co-ordination for public management improvement; organisation, public personnel policy, citizen-administration relations, and information technology	
Ministry of the Interior	– decentralisation and deconcentration; improvements in autonomy of local government	
Ministry of National Economy	– public enterprise management; regulatory policy for the private sector	
Ministry of Finance	– civil service pay; budgeting; financial management systems	

IRELAND

Programme for Economic and Social Progress

A new comprehensive agreement was signed by the Government and the social partners (employers, trade unions, farming interests). The Programme provides a strategic framework for the next decade with specific proposals for the initial years (1991-93) on:

- macro-economic stability policies, geared to low inflation, low interest rates and reduction of the national debt;
- a programme of fundamental structural reforms, especially a continuation of radical tax reform begun under the Programme for National Recovery, a major assault on long-term unemployment and a restructuring of social services, in particular social welfare, the health services, education and housing; and
- incorporating a formal national agreement on moderate pay increases between the Irish Congress of Trade Unions and employer organisations.

Administrative budgets for line departments

Three-year administrative budgets for the period 1991-93 were introduced in most departments of the civil service with the objectives of:

- reducing the cost of running each line department by 2 per cent in 1992 and a further 2 per cent in 1993 in constant 1991 terms; and
- improving efficiency and effectiveness in each department through:
  - delegating greater authority from the Minister for Finance to line departments in relation to administrative expenditure and related matters; and
  - encouraging and facilitating the delegation of greater authority to individual line managers in departments in relation to administrative expenditure.

These budgets are in operation in 23 departments employing some 22 000 staff, or 80 per cent of the civil service. The total expenditure involved is Ir£ 560 million in 1991 terms.

Financial management systems

A financial management system (FMS) software package was selected in 1991 to support the financial management needs of most departments. The need for a computerised FMS was accelerated by the introduction of the three-year administrative budgets. The FMS software package, which had to be partially modified, is now operational in one department and will be installed in several others in the early months of 1992.

Management of human resources

An initiative to place renewed emphasis on, and to adopt, a better planned and more coherent approach to staff training and development was endorsed by the heads of departments in the civil service in mid-1991. The initiative provides for a strategic approach to staff development which is work-centred and linked to organisational objectives, operational plans and the needs of individuals. The preparation of staff development plans and training programmes based on needs-analysis surveys is to be promoted. One such analysis in a department will be completed shortly and will provide a "model" for the conduct of similar analyses in other departments. The initiative is also being supported centrally through the preparation and promulgation of a code of standards and guidelines on best training practices and the establishment of a fund to subvent innovative training initiatives and developments.

FACTSHEET: IRELAND

A. PRINCIPAL RECENT PUBLIC MANAGEMENT DEVELOPMENTS

1985:
- White Paper "Serving the Country Better" published.
- Decentralised, planning-driven approach to IT established.

1987:
- Budget goals defined to contain public expenditure in real terms at or below 1986 levels as a percentage of GNP.
- Department of Public Service merged with Department of Finance which takes leading role in public management reform.
- Embargo on recruitment introduced across public service and programme of enhanced early retirement announced.
- Government accepts in principle a report by an independent Review Body on Higher Remuneration in the Public Sector which recommends that the pay of a senior management grade (Assistant Secretary) be performance-related.
- Government announces programme to relocate some 3 000 civil servants from Dublin to 12 regional centres.

1988:
- Comprehensive three-year agreement with public service unions negotiated.
- Programme initiated to review statutory and information requirements which affect business and industry.

1989:
- Department of Finance survey of public offices to identify if adequate standards of privacy for client interviews being used and if suitably qualified staff being employed.
- In budget statement, Minister for Finance announces new system of budgetary allocations for administrative or running costs based on a three-year period and on delegated spending authority.
- Review of the role of the Comptroller and Auditor General by Department of Finance.
- Efficiency Audit Group created to examine practices of government departments and to make recommendations for reducing costs and enhancing efficiency.

1989/90:
- A further 1 200 civil servants moved from Dublin to regional centres.

1990:
- Filling of essential posts authorised but no general resumption in public service recruitment.
- Performance-related pay scheme introduced for Assistant Secretary grade.
- Country-wide Government Telecommunications Network launched to improve communications and support decentralisation.

B. INSTITUTIONAL RESPONSIBILITY FOR PUBLIC MANAGEMENT IMPROVEMENT

ORGANISATION	TASKS AND RESPONSIBILITIES	OTHER INFORMATION
Department of Finance	– overall responsibility for public management reforms – monitoring performance of departments	In 1987, the Department of the Public Service was merged with the Department of Finance. An Efficiency Audit Group was established in 1989. It includes representatives from the Department of Finance and the Department of the Taoiseach (Prime Minister), and prominent businessmen from the private sector (one of whom is the Group Chairman). Its task is to examine the operations of government departments.

ITALY

The year 1991 was an eventful one for the Italian public administration in many ways, following a year of intense and important regulatory production. Mention should be made of Law No. 125 of 10 April 1991 concerning "positive action to achieve equality between men and women at work", which complemented existing regulation and at the same time made a link with specific European Community regulations. Other initiatives of great importance in 1991 were:

- the application and "fine-tuning" of recent laws (No. 142/90 on local autonomy; No. 146/90 on the right to strike; and especially No. 241/90 on administrative transparency); and
- the launching of a **global strategy** which strengthens the integration and co-ordination of civil service issues within the national system.

The latter is particularly important, given the approach of the Single European Market. Examples of its repercussions are the laws concerning reform of the financial administration (No. 358 of 29 October 1991) and administrative reform of the Treasury (No. 370 of 27 November 1991).

An important result of this global strategy – which also considers major questions like the costs of labour, retirement, and taxation – is the bill concerning labour, employment, and collective bargaining for public servants. This bill was proposed by the Government, with consensus from the social partners, and was approved by the Council of Ministers on 16 January 1992 with support from the Minister for the Public Service.

This bill goes beyond the provisions of the outline law on public employment (Law No. 93 of 28 March 1988) by specifying that the regulation of the legal and economic status of public servants can be negotiated with the trade unions – exceptions being made for regulation of particular aspects and for specific categories of staff such as senior public servants ("alti dirigenti").

The other particularly important aspect of this bill is the proposed creation of an "agency for trade union relations within the public administration" which would represent government agencies in collective bargaining at the national level and would assist in decentralised bargaining, according to directives issued by the President of the Council of Ministers.

FACTSHEET: ITALY

A. PRINCIPAL RECENT PUBLIC MANAGEMENT DEVELOPMENTS

1980: – Abolition of promotion system for careers based on qualifications.

1983: – Ministry of the Public Service established to co-ordinate management of human resources and use of IT across the public service.
– Implementation of a privatisation policy involving complete State withdrawal from some sectors.

1984: – Law passed requiring promotion to "managerial career group" by examination.

1988: – Legislative changes made to restructure the public administration including re-organisation of the Presidency of the Council of Ministers and of the Government Accounting Office.
– Council of the Presidency set up with direct impact on the Court of Auditors.
– New law on public service linked to the Finance Act and providing for staff mobility to improve efficiency.

1989: – New medium-term fiscal programme designed to reduce public sector borrowing, introduce multi-year expenditure plans and support the recruitment freeze.
– Circular of the Minister for the Public Service launches a project to define and evaluate performance of the public administration and to better identify staff needs.

1990: – Project launched on "Functionality and Efficiency of the Public Administration".
– New legislation on relations between the administration and citizens concerning transparency, simplification, consultation and rights of access to documents.
– New legislation on local autonomy and co-operation between regions, provinces and communes.
– New regulations introduced governing the right to strike in essential public services.

B.   INSTITUTIONAL RESPONSIBILITY FOR PUBLIC MANAGEMENT IMPROVEMENT

ORGANISATION	TASKS AND RESPONSIBILITIES	OTHER INFORMATION
Presidency of the Council of Ministers	– general guidelines and co-ordination – definition of general and sectoral policies	
Ministry of the Public Service	– co-ordination of public management initiatives – introduction of office automation and co-ordination of IT use – planning of recruitment – collective agreements with the unions (salaries, etc.) – control of efficiency and evaluation of work performance	Established in 1983. It has a policy advisory role, while all financial responsibility lies with the Treasury.
Ministry of the Treasury – Government Accounting Office (Ragioneria Generale dello Stato)	– guidance and control of public expenditures – co-ordination of new financial and economic legislation and of plans for managerial organisation (personnel matters) – definition of legislative measures regarding revenues and expenditures – collecting and updating public sector accounts – review of reforms of the accounting system and of the preparation of the budget – inspection and audit of public bodies	
Ministry of Finance	– guidance and application of tax procedures for budget revenues – systematic control of the implementation of tax procedures – support for budgetary policy orientation – performance of the tax system; measurement of real fiscal returns (fight against tax evasion and tax fraud)	

JAPAN

The third **Provisional Council for the Promotion of Administrative Reform** was established by law in October 1990 for a three-year term. The Council is an advisory body to the Prime Minister. It performs the following functions:

- submitting its "opinions" to the Prime Minister on its own initiative; and
- presenting its "reports" as requested by the Prime Minister.

Both "opinions" and "reports" are based on the results of its examination and deliberation on the progress of reform of important matters (pertaining to the improvement of administrative systems and operations) as recommended by the Provisional Commission for Administrative Reform (1981-83) and the first and second Provisional Councils for the Promotion of Administrative Reform (1983-86 and 1987-90). The Prime Minister is required by law to pay respect to the opinions and reports of the Council.

At the first meeting of the Council held in October 1990, the Prime Minister requested the Council to examine the following three subjects:

- **progress of reforms** based on the reports and opinions of the Provisional Commission for Administrative Reform and of the first and second Provisional Councils for the Promotion of Administrative Reform;
- **measures to be taken** to enrich the quality of people's lives and to cope with internationalisation of the Japanese society and public administration;
- provision of a **uniform legal system of administrative procedures** to increase transparency and to ensure fairness.

So far the Council has submitted **three opinions** ("The Opinion concerning Administrative Reform in Formulating the Budget of FY 1991"; the same for FY 1992; and "The Opinion on the Progress of Administrative Reform") and **four reports.**

"The First Report on Administrative Reform: Promoting Internationalisation and Improving the Quality of Life" was submitted in July 1991. Specific issues dealt with in this report were: the goals and the direction of reform needed to achieve an "affluent" life as well as the abatement of over-concentration in the Tokyo metropolitan area; the vitalisation of the provinces or local areas, and the establishment of self-sustaining municipalities; and the basic principles of Japanese external policies and administrative structures to promote them.

"The Second Report on Administrative Reform: Promoting Internationalisation and Improving the Quality of Life" was submitted in December 1991. This report elaborated further the same themes dealt with in the First Report and made specific recommendations on the reform of development assistance administration, conservation of global environment, regional welfare systems, education, and so on.

In September 1991, "The Report on the Basic Measures to Correct Unfair Securities and Finance Business Practices" was submitted in response to a series of securities and finance scandals such as loss compensation by securities companies. In this report, the Council recommended that the Government establish an independent inspection body within the Ministry of Finance. The new agency is tentatively named in the report as "the Securities and Finance Inspection Commission" and is expected mainly to watch and ensure that market participants – including securities companies and banks – abide by the rules and regulations in the market.

In December 1991, "The Report on the Fair and Transparent Administrative Procedure" was submitted. In this report, the Council recommended the enactment of a general and common administrative procedure law.

Organisational and structural change: Devolution to local governments

The present efforts towards devolution in the government are based on the Cabinet decision, "The Platform for the Promotion of Reform concerning the Relationship between the National and Local Governments". This Cabinet decision was made in December 1989 in response to the report and recommendation of the Provisional Council for the Promotion of Administrative Reform. The Government prepared a package bill of amendments of laws for devolution to the local governments and submitted it to the Diet. The bill was enacted in April 1991.

Management of human resources

A new personnel reduction plan (the eighth) was decided by the Cabinet in July 1991, the previous one being scheduled to end in March 1992. The new plan sets the target for personnel reductions during the five years from FY 1992 at 39 048 (or 4.52 per cent of the total central government personnel at the end of FY 1991).

Better quality service delivery and client satisfaction

To achieve a kinder, more sincere public service, the Government made a Cabinet decision entitled **"Refreshing Administrative Service Movement"** in January 1988. This has been continuously enforced as part of a nation-wide administrative reform effort involving government agencies and public corporations and with the co-operation of local governments.

"The Act for the Protection of Personal Data held by Administrative Organs" was enacted in December 1988 and fully enforced in October 1990.

Regulatory review and reform

The present efforts for deregulation in government are based on the Cabinet decision, "The Platform for the Promotion of Deregulation", made in December 1988. According to the third follow-up report of the Platform, made public in November 1991, most of the programmes in the Platform have been implemented, including legislation such as an amendment to the "Large-scale Retail Store Law".

Monitoring and evaluation

Follow-up of the promotion of administrative reform: The Management and Co-ordination Agency reviews the progress of reform based on the reports and recommendations of the Provisional Commission for Administrative Reform and the Provisional Council for the Promotion of Administrative Reform, in order to promote administrative reform and to contribute to the activities of the Council. The Agency also promotes the implementation of such Cabinet decisions relevant to administrative reform as the Platform for the Promotion of Deregulation and the Platform for the Promotion of Reform concerning the Relationship between the National and Local Governments, as mentioned above.

Administrative inspection: To contribute to the improvement of the operations of administrative organs and programmes, the Management and Co-ordination Agency conducts administrative inspections in which the Agency investigates the operation of government agencies, makes analyses and evaluations of programmes based on the facts or evidence gained through investigations, and makes recommendations to the agencies concerned. In FY 1990, 17 inspection programmes were completed. Recommendations were made in areas such as housing administration, and 20 new inspection programmes were launched.

FACTSHEET: JAPAN

A. PRINCIPAL RECENT PUBLIC MANAGEMENT DEVELOPMENTS

1981: – March: Inauguration of the Provisional Commission for Administrative Reform (PCAR) (expiration of its term in March 1983).

1982: – September: Cabinet Decision on the Fundamental Principle of Administrative Reform to implement the Third Report of the PCAR.

1983: – May: Cabinet Decision on the New Fundamental Principle of Administrative Reform to implement the Final Report of the PCAR.
– July: Inauguration of the first Provisional Council for the Promotion of Administrative Reform (PCPAR) (expiration of its term in June 1986).

1984: – January: Cabinet Decision on the Fundamental Principle of Administrative Reform of FY 1984. (The Cabinet has been making a decision on the principle of administrative reform every year since then.)
– July: Inauguration of the Management and Co-ordination Agency.

1985: – April: Privatisation of Nippon Telegram and Telephone Public Corporation and Nippon Tobacco and Salt Public Corporation.

1986: – July: Re-organisation of the Cabinet Secretariat and establishment of Security Council.
– August: Cabinet Decision on the seventh personnel reduction plan.

1987: – April: Division and privatisation of Japanese National Railways.
– April: Inauguration of the second Provisional Council for the Promotion of Administrative Reform (expiration of its term in April 1990).

1988: – December: Cabinet Decision on the Platform for the Promotion of Deregulation.

1989: – December: Cabinet Decision on the Platform for the Promotion of Reform concerning the Relationship between the National and Local Governments.

1990: – October: Inauguration of the third Provisional Council for the Promotion of Administrative Reform (expiration of its term in October 1993).

1991: – July: Cabinet Decision on the eighth personnel reduction plan.

B. INSTITUTIONAL RESPONSIBILITY FOR PUBLIC MANAGEMENT IMPROVEMENT

ORGANISATION	TASKS AND RESPONSIBILITIES	OTHER INFORMATION
Prime Minister's Office – Management and Co-ordination Agency	– personnel management (co-ordination and integration of policies and programmes, etc., developed by ministries and agencies for personnel management of their own national public employees, etc.) – management of administrative organisation – control of total staff numbers – administrative inspection	Set up in 1984 to co-ordinate government functions.
Cabinet Secretariat	– co-ordination function for government policy	
National Personnel Authority	– personnel management (recruitment, remuneration, training, working conditions, grievance procedure, etc.)	An independent agency reporting to the Cabinet.

LUXEMBOURG

Management of human resources

Since 1990, particularly with the enactment of a law on 12 December, public servants and public employees benefit from an end-of-year allowance which corresponds to 50 per cent of the base salary for the month of December. The same law also increased the salaries of public servants who entered State service after 1 January 1989, and increased by 2.5 per cent the base index for salaries and pensions for all public servants, retroactively from 1 January 1990.

This law was enacted following a **wage agreement** negotiated between the General Public Service Confederation, which is the representative public service trade union, and the Minister for the Public Service. The agreement was signed on 28 September 1990.

At present, several major projects relative to the public service are being debated in the Council of Ministers. One of the proposed reforms involves a complete **restructuring of the professional training** currently offered by the Institute of Administrative Training and the State services.

A proposition has also been put forward to regulate the **promotion schemes** for various careers along uniform lines, with precise criteria and with more emphasis on the continuing development of the personnel.

FACTSHEET: LUXEMBOURG

A. PRINCIPAL RECENT PUBLIC MANAGEMENT DEVELOPMENTS

1983:   –   Creation of the Institute of Administrative Training to provide initial and continuing training for public servants.

1986:   –   Legislation passed to emphasise automatic promotion in the public service after a number of years in lower grades.

1990:   –   Government policy to equip all public services with IT and hence promote optimum management of human and material resources.

B. INSTITUTIONAL RESPONSIBILITY FOR PUBLIC MANAGEMENT IMPROVEMENT

ORGANISATION	TASKS AND RESPONSIBILITIES	OTHER INFORMATION
Ministry for the Public Service	– administrative reform, in particular office automation and computerised personnel management	Follows instructions on organisation of ministerial departments as set out in a Grand-Ducal Decree of 1989.
Public Personnel Administration – Division for Administrative Organisation	– advises on projects for (re-)organisation of management staff in public services and public establishments under State control, in particular on harmonisation and co-ordination – prepares medium/long-term administrative reform projects following Government guidelines – collects statistics on public personnel – provides secretariat support to the Administration	
Commission on Economy and Rationalisation	– proposes measures to reduce size of the public service and to rationalise working methods – proposes cuts of abusive or excessive expenditure	Created in 1974.

NETHERLANDS

Policy context and goals

The major goal of the Dutch Government regarding public administration in recent years has been to limit public sector employment and expenditure to specific boundaries in order to reduce the budget deficit. Linked with this is the objective of improving the quality of public services. The slogan is: "Fewer civil servants but a better service." In the 1990s, these goals are to be furthered by three big operations:

- a "normalisation" process of civil service labour conditions;
- a "decentralisation impulse"; and
- the "great efficiency operation".

The progressive European unification process was very important in the second half of 1991, when the Dutch Government held the presidency that led to the Treaty of Maastricht (European Political Union).

Organisational and structural change

The process of **privatisation** and the creation of **independent agencies** have progressed along two main lines. First, the Government adopted the recommendations of the working group for the review of management rules contained in the report "Towards More Result-oriented Management". This report attempted to steer a middle course between the need for management at the macro level and the scope for greater authority at the micro level. It made a number of proposals concerning the introduction of agencies in order to widen the range of forms of self-management. Agencies are more independent parts of the civil service, and are considered to be ideally suited for ensuring that the emphasis is shifted from resource-oriented authorisation to performance-oriented accountability. Agencies typically have greater managerial powers and responsibilities than "normal" civil service departments – for example, broader facilities for handling the budget, possibly in combination with accrual accounting and commercial bookkeeping.

Secondly, the **decentralisation** issue attracted the renewed attention of the Government in 1991. The Government gave fresh impetus to the devolution of responsibilities and resources to lower tiers of government. This programme has led to an extensive package of proposals. The number of specific payments and the volume of regulations and various obligations which lower tiers of government still have at present will decrease (e.g. the submission of plans). Through the "decentralisation impulse", several central government tasks will be given to municipalities, provinces and regional bodies, at the same time producing savings of Gld 500 million.

A strong relationship exists between the **Single European Market** developments and the renewed debate on restructuring and strengthening the big cities in a regional setting and perhaps even merging the Dutch provinces according to a more European scale. Decentralisation to these new entities must make them more competitive and effective in order to perform their infrastructural tasks better, and to facilitate the functioning of the distribution and financial sectors of the economy where the Netherlands expects to produce economic growth.

Management of policy-making

The developments mentioned above have enhanced a core business operation for the central government, generally referred to as the **"great efficiency operation".** The Dutch Government planned this operation for the years 1991-94, as a successor of the "slimming-down operation". With this latest initiative, the Dutch Government intends to improve the quality and the efficiency of the central administration. The operation started with an attempt to define for each ministry what is its "core business", and raises the question of which central tasks must be performed. This operation must result in a reduction in personnel expenditures of Gld 660 million and a reduction of about 9 000 jobs by 1994. One of the instruments used in this respect is the analysis of the core tasks of each ministry in order to make selections of tasks. The Dutch Parliament has started debates on possible transformations in the structure of the governing bodies of the country, i.e. Parliament, the government itself, and the ministries.

Better quality service delivery and client satisfaction

Within the Dutch public administration, attempts are being made to increase substantially the **accessibility of government information,** and to prevent the situation where a civilian is expected to produce all his/her personal facts through computerisation whenever contact is made with a government body. It has for example been decided to restructure the organisation of the Dutch taxation authorities. The internal structure currently based on separate tax laws will be based on client groups, irrespective of the applicability of the different tax laws.

Furthermore, experiments have been launched to concentrate contacts between the government on the one hand and civilians and private sector companies on the other. These experiments relate to the integration of counter and desk functions of different government bodies following the principle of **"civic service centres".**

Financial management, and monitoring and evaluation

In 1986, the **"financial accountability operation"** was launched. The basic aim is that every ministry should bear primary responsibility for the structure and organisation of its own accounting system, with the Minister of Finance playing a co-ordinating and supervisory role. The chief objectives of the operation are:

- to establish an accounting system in the ministries which permits efficient and legitimate implementation of budgets, incorporating both commitments and cash disbursements;
- to ensure that auditors' reports cover the whole of a ministerial accounting system and that the rendering of accounts is accompanied by a favourable auditor's report;
- to establish a system for the supply of financial information between the various ministries and the Ministry of Finance and between the civil service and Parliament so that information on budgetary preparation, implementation and accounts can be provided rapidly and efficiently; and
- to adjust the structure and presentation of draft budgets, supplementary budgets, accounts and budgetary statements so that Parliament is better able to exercise its right to approve the budget and its right of authorisation. Both the 1976 Government Accounts Act and regulations deriving from it will be amended.

The financial accountability operation neared completion in 1991. As a result of this operation, management can be made increasingly subservient to policy, and greater attention can be devoted to the **efficiency** of the civil service.

Management of human resources: Normalisation

Significant steps were taken in 1991 to further the aim to transform the government employer to a "normal" one. Historically, the State-employer and its administration have a special character. Without harming this special status, several elements from the market sector can be introduced in management and personnel policy to meet the increasing demands of society for quality products from government. Important elements in this strategy are the normalisation of labour relations (consultation and negotiation procedures, rights to strike), of pay conditions, of labour market policy, and of management (efficiency and labour productivity).

The focal point in the review of the consultation procedure on labour conditions is the way in which the negotiations on pay, pensions and related matters are being conducted (the 1989 **"Proto-col"**). In the 1980s, the employer could – if no agreement was possible, eventually in the capacity of legislator – unilaterally determine the conditions of employment. The aim of former "consultation" related only to a positive commitment to reach an agreement; it implied a dialogue, an exchange of arguments, a willingness to reconsider initial positions between the government and the staff represen-tatives. The protocol, on the other hand, is to be regarded as one step further, i.e. the requirement to reach an agreement (*conditio sine qua non*). In other words, in the 1990s, for the introduction or alteration of regulations from which individual employees may derive rights (except for legal social security matters), and also job-creation measures which limit the budget margin for pay and conditions, an agreement with the majority of the relevant trade union federations is required.

The possibilities for lower tiers of government to formulate and execute their own **decentral-ised personnel policies** have been increased. It is the aim of the Minister of the Interior to introduce step by step (from 1992 onwards) a completely decentralised consultation structure, including general salary adjustment and labour time. In 1991, however, no agreement was reached with the unions in this respect. Staff consultation procedures and the right to strike will be codified in conformity with private sector arrangements, except for defence personnel.

In the field of **management development,** the stimulation of mobility has regained momentum. Mobility of top managers in the civil service will be organised from a central co-ordination unit, managed by a supervisory board of secretaries-general. For the lower levels, intra-ministerial networks are being created to further mobility. The concept of a general appointment in the Dutch civil service will be introduced.

The policy to increase the number of civil servants from **minority groups** in Dutch society has been pursued with increased effort, aiming at 5 per cent minorities working in the Dutch civil service by 1995. By the end of 1993, the central government will also employ 5 per cent handicapped persons in the civil service. The policies concerning women are directed at increasing the movement of female civil servants to the higher ranks.

Top priority was given in 1991 to **reducing the sick rate and the consequential absenteeism** and the numbers of civil servants falling under the disablement act. This absenteeism is to be reduced by 0.5 per cent each year. In these fields, specific targets have been formulated by the Cabinet. At the same time, means and measures (including pay deductions) are being developed in pilot projects by the National Health Service, the National Psychological Service, and the National Training Institute (all to be privatised in the early 1990s) under the leadership of the Ministry of the Interior and supported by legislation to assist management in reaching the targets.

Regulatory review and reform

On 4 March 1991, the Minister of Justice presented to Parliament his paper "Zicht op Wetgeving" (Perspective on Law). In this paper, it is indicated how the government can prevent shortcomings in legislation and how laws can be made more consistent. Important actions are:

- In early phases, more attention will be given to the practical problems of execution and maintenance of law.
- All laws will be checked by the Justice Department.
- In cases where laws have substantial societal consequences, a specific commission (the Kortmann Commission) will be consulted.
- A sub-group of that Commission will advise on the European aspects of Dutch legislation.

FACTSHEET: NETHERLANDS

A. PRINCIPAL RECENT PUBLIC MANAGEMENT DEVELOPMENTS

1982-86:   –   Comprehensive government re-organisation project including decentralisation measures, especially in personnel management.

1984:   –   Provision made to award bonus payments in recognition of special effort.
       –   Government decision to transfer competences to lower level line managers and to decentralise responsibility for many aspects of staffing policy.

1984-86:   –   Central steering committee on personnel policy monitors project for re-organisation of all personnel management.

1988:   –   A market-related allowance or bonus to recruit and retain certain categories of civil servants (with skills in demand) was introduced in order to respond to specific needs.
       –   Ministry of Home Affairs asks universities to organise a management training programme for young civil servants.

1988-90:   –   Targets set for job reductions for each ministry with a 1988 target of 3 500 cuts and a total target of approximately 20 000 full-time equivalents.

1989:   –   System of pay differentials introduced across the public service to reward performance with approximately 23 million guilders earmarked for civil service funding.
       –   School of Public Administration founded to improve training of management staff.
       –   Management Development Advice Centre established under the auspices of the Ministry of Home Affairs.
       –   The requirement to reach an agreement on labour conditions for civil servants was institutionalised (protocol).

1990:   –   Preparations start for introducing the concept of "labour productivity in the public sector".
       –   Ministerial committee formed to steer a "large-scale efficiency operation" aimed at reducing government tasks, improving structural organisation and a cost-reduction of 300 million guilders by 1994.
       –   "Small-scale efficiency operation" launched with the aim of increasing labour productivity in the public sector by the same percentage as in comparable private sector activities.

1991:   –   Government announced draft legislation to Parliament that will give civil servants the right to strike.

B. INSTITUTIONAL RESPONSIBILITY FOR PUBLIC MANAGEMENT IMPROVEMENT

ORGANISATION	TASKS AND RESPONSIBILITIES	OTHER INFORMATION
Ministry of Home Affairs		
– Directorate General for Management and Personnel Policy (DGMP)	– co-ordination of personnel policy; salary negotiations, number of posts, job descriptions, training and staff development – initiation of modernisation schemes (e.g. decentralisation and management development)	
– Directorate General for Public Administration (DGOB)	– overall responsibility for the "great efficiency operation" and the decentralisation of central government tasks	
Ministry of Finance	– financial management; control of re-organisation	

NEW ZEALAND

Organisational and structural change

During 1991, major changes to social policy were announced. There are significant consequential changes being implemented in the structure and organisation of social policy agencies. The major changes announced were as follows:

- Abolition of Area Health Boards and their replacement by four Regional Health Authorities. New Crown Health Enterprises and Community Trusts to deliver services are also to be established. Public health issues are to be handled by a new Public Health Commission. This Commission will also oversee a new Public Health Agency responsible for policy and funding.
- The conversion of the Housing Corporation into a State-owned Enterprise (SOE) and the establishment of a new Ministry of Housing as a policy agency.
- The winding up of the Iwi Transition Agency and Manatu Maori and their replacement by a new Ministry of Maori Development.

In areas other than social policy, the science activities formerly conducted within departments are being restructured as Crown Research Institutes and a new Civil Aviation Authority is to be set up. The Traffic Safety Service, currently part of the Ministry of Transport, is to be merged with the Police.

Management of policy-making

Changes have been made within the Department of Prime Minister and Cabinet to enhance policy co-ordination. New units in this Department will oversee the health policy changes. The use of joint private and public sector task forces to develop major policy initiatives has continued.

Better quality service delivery and client satisfaction

Both the Inland Revenue Department and the Department of Social Welfare are introducing new computer systems to process the huge number of transactions handled by each department. The intention is to speed up processing and improve accuracy.

Financial management

The reforms introduced by the Public Finance Act 1989 have continued to be bedded into government reporting systems. 1991/92 will be the first financial year where all departments will have had a full year's history on the new accrual accounting systems and reporting on outputs. 1991 also saw the introduction of a capital charge on all departments to reflect the cost of capital used by departments in the prices of their outputs. 1991/92 will see the tabling of the first set of accrual-based financial statements for the New Zealand Government.

Regulatory review and reform

Major changes to labour market regulation were introduced with the passage of the Employment Contracts Act 1991. This legislation places more emphasis upon individual employment contracts than the 1987 Labour Relations Act.

Monitoring and evaluation

A major review of the state sector reforms introduced since 1987 was conducted and completed in 1991, as requested by the Minister of State Services on behalf of the Government. The Government has acknowledged in the wake of State sector reform legislation that it is important for departments not to operate as businesses in complete isolation from one another. It believes it is important that managers at all levels re-establish inter-departmental channels of communication and formal links to prevent a loss of the emphasis on the collective interest of Government. The review is structured into four main areas:

- accountability and the collective interest;
- achieving improved departmental performance;
- the cost benefits of compliance with reporting and audit requirements; and
- improving the quality of senior management in the public sector.

Employment Contracts Act

The most significant recent development in State sector human resource management has been the introduction of the **Employment Contracts Act 1991.** The Act, which came into force on 15 May 1991, replaces the previous employment statute, the Labour Relations Act 1987, and creates a new legal and institutional framework for the practice of industrial relations. The Act applies to the State sector as well as to the private sector, though the statutory responsibility of the State Services Commission (SSC) to negotiate collectively bargained conditions for the Public, Health and Education Services is preserved. Briefly, the key features of the Employment Contracts Act are described below.

All employment contracts are covered by the provisions of the Act, and the institutions established by it – the Employment Tribunal and the Employment Court – have exclusive jurisdiction in all matters concerning employment contracts.

The Act removes the special status in law of registered trade unions and allows employees the choice of whether or not to belong to any form of employees organisation (which may include unions) formed to represent their interests. Any arrangements that require employees to belong or not to belong to an employees organisation, or that discriminate on those grounds, are unlawful.

Previous union rights of automatic industrial representation guaranteed through registration have been abolished and employees and employers are able to choose who will represent them, either individually or collectively, in negotiations. The number, type, and mix of contracts to apply in a particular workplace are a negotiable matter. Employers and employees are free to negotiate about whether to have individual or collective contracts, and – subject to the Act and other legislation – their content.

Employment contracts apply only to the parties on whose behalf they are negotiated, although bargaining agents may become parties to those contracts subject to the agreement of the employer(s) and employee(s) concerned. New employees may also become parties to an existing collective contract where the contract contains a clause allowing them to do so, and where the employee and the employer agree. However, there is no requirement for them to do so. Once agreed, contracts are binding on the parties to them, and although they may be varied by agreement during their term, strikes or lockouts during this period are generally unlawful, except on the grounds of safety or health. Employees or employers may enforce their contracts themselves or may authorise an agent to act for them. This need not be the same agent who represents them in bargaining.

Personal grievance and disputes rights and procedures are extended to all employees, irrespective of whether they are employed under individual or collective employment contracts. All employment contracts must provide effective procedures for the settlement of grievances arising over unjustifiable dismissals, discrimination, sexual harassment, duress, or disadvantageous treatment in employment, and of disputes about the interpretation, application, or operation of employment contracts.

A specialist **Employment Tribunal** is created by the Act to provide mediation services and to adjudicate on matters concerning employment contracts. The Tribunal deals with disputes, personal grievances, other breaches of employment contracts, and breaches of parts of the Act and certain other legislation. An **Employment Court** is also established to hear appeals from decisions of the Tribunal, as well as to hear and determine other matters under the Act that fall within its jurisdiction. Principally, these concern matters arising from the Act's provisions for freedom of association and sanctity of contract, though the Court is able to deal with any action founded on an employment contract.

Decentralisation of bargaining authority

Although the SSC is, at law, the employer party for the purposes of negotiating collective employment contracts in the Public, Health and Education Services, it has the power to delegate this authority to individual employers in each sector. Given the expertise gained by departments to date, the SSC has decided to delegate its bargaining authority to public service chief executives for the 1992 wage round. The delegation is, however, subject to negotiations being conducted in accordance with Government policy and the agreed parameters for the round, and an SSC representative will be required to be present at all negotiations.

Under an amendment made to the State Sector Act in 1989, the SSC's role in negotiating collective employment contracts in the tertiary education sector (Universities, Polytechnics, and Colleges of Education) will fully devolve to the chief executives of those institutions on 1 January 1992. A further amendment to the State Sector Act, made as a consequence of the Employment Contracts Act, has removed the SSC's ability to participate in negotiations in this sector after this date, and replaced it with a consultative role only.

Performance pay

Performance-based pay regimes were introduced to the public service in 1988 as part of a move away from the previous national pay system toward a more comprehensive remuneration structure for departments, better suited to the new decentralised industrial environment. A centrepiece of this has been the establishment of a system of ranges of rates of remuneration.

Ranges of rates structures fix upper and lower limits on pay, but movement within these is relatively flexibly determined, and is not confined to fixed salary steps or incremental steps or progression. Because they are focused on the position holder rather than the job itself, pay and progression can be related more closely to performance, as well as to specific person requirements and recruitment and retention factors. Most departments have, however, retained some elements of incremental progression in salary structures, usually at entry and lower ranges.

While it is difficult to make precise judgements about the **costs or benefits** of performance pay regimes at this stage, a number of concerns have been raised about the functioning of performance pay systems. Wage drift in particular has appeared to have been one consequence of the new system, highlighting the need for effective job evaluation, performance appraisal and internal control and audit systems. Problems of administrative complexity have also been identified.

Public administration

In 1990 the SSC issued a *Public Service Code of Conduct*, detailing minimum standards of integrity and conduct expected of public servants in their work. This publication has recently been complemented by *Public Service and the Public Servant,* a booklet of essays on the wider constitutional and "ethical" issues involved in public service administrative practice. It is expected that these essays will form the basis for a more definitive set of guidelines on such matters in due course.

State sector superannuation

The Government has announced its intention to close the current service-wide Government Superannuation Fund (GSF) to new members after 30 June 1992, and has commenced a process of review of future State sector superannuation policy. A review of the various subschemes of the GSF (such as those applying to the Police, Armed Forces, and prison officers) has also been initiated. Key issues in this include the large unfunded liabilities that have been built up by the GSF over time (some NZ$ 8-11 billion), the severe fiscal constraints on State spending generally and State employers in particular, and the Government's desire, as an employer, to provide appropriate superannuation arrangements for its employees in this context.

FACTSHEET: NEW ZEALAND

A.   PRINCIPAL RECENT PUBLIC MANAGEMENT DEVELOPMENTS

1987:
- "Corporatisation" of departments producing goods and services into state-owned enterprises aimed at encouraging a more business-like approach.
- Restructuring of government departments to separate policy advice and operational functions.
- Intention to reform the local government system announced.

1988:
- State Sector Act introduces policy goals for major public sector reform with main aims of enhancing efficient and effective public sector management by increasing managerial autonomy and more clearly defining accountabilities; preserving the values of service to the community and integrity; and ensuring that the State is a "good employer".
- Budget announces public sector financial management reforms including new budget cycle and performance agreements with department heads (Chief Executives).
- Privatisation programme implemented through the sale of some major government assets and also applied to departmental trading activities to increase efficiency and reduce government debt.

1989:
- Public Finance Act clarifies the relationship between outputs and outcomes, the distinction between Crown as owner and purchaser, and alternative modes of appropriation (based on either accrual accounting or revolving funds).
- Local government reform introduced with reduction in number of local authorities from over 600 to 94, better relating them to local and regional communities of interest, making them more accountable, and enabling them to provide services more efficiently.
- Introduction of a comprehensive bill to reform resource management and allocate responsibility for implementation to restructured regional government.
- State Services Commission restructured to focus on servicing ministers rather than other departments.
- Structure of Prime Minister's Office and Cabinet Office reviewed with aim of improving co-ordination and quality of advice provided.
- State Sector Act amended to further extend reform principles to the wider education sector and other State services and to reflect the restructuring of the State Services Commission.

1990:
- By end of year all of current core public sector bodies moved to new financial management system (i.e. outputs adequately specified and agreed between ministers; operating full accrual accounting and cash arrangement systems; and able to meet new financial reporting requirements).

1991:
- Introduction of Employment Contracts Act 1991 provides new legal and institutional arrangements for private and public sector industrial relations. The role of the State Services Commission in negotiating collectively bargained conditions of employment in the core State sector is maintained, but the process of delegation of bargaining authority commences in the public service.

B.   INSTITUTIONAL RESPONSIBILITY FOR PUBLIC MANAGEMENT IMPROVEMENT

ORGANISATION	TASKS AND RESPONSIBILITIES	OTHER INFORMATION
State Services Commission (SSC)	- promote and co-ordinate the implementation of the State Sector Act - review departmental and Chief Executive performance - issue a code of conduct covering minimum standards of integrity and conduct - provide, maintain and develop the Senior Executive Service	The State Sector Act of 1988 announced a managerial modernisation based on decentralisation. It changed the role of the SSC from detailed implementation to broader monitoring and developing of government policies. Senior executives are appointed for limited terms on performance-based contracts.
Treasury	- financial reform	

NORWAY

Organisational and structural change

A new organisational form, State-owned enterprise (statsforetak), has been established through Parliament's passing of a new act. Several existing public enterprises are, or have been, under consideration for re-organisation into the new model. It has been decided to transform the present Statkraft (State Power Systems) into two separate State-owned enterprises.

A report on **guidelines** for the use of boards of public agencies, enterprises, companies and foundations has been presented by a Royal Commission. The report proposes criteria for when to use boards, what their tasks, powers and responsibilities should be, and measures for improving the composition of boards.

An expert group has presented a report on the potential for increased **cost-effectiveness** in the public sector. Provision of public goods and services, regulated sectors, and sectors subject to public transfer payments are reviewed in the report. The Government has initiated cost-effectiveness scrutinies within selected areas: education, culture, communication, and internal administration.

During 1991, several major projects on **restructuring and re-organising** the civil service were launched. Reforms have been adopted, proposed, or are under review within, *inter alia*: the State Health Administration (especially the Directorate of Health); the Police Administration; the Taxes, Customs and Excise Administration; the State's industrial and regional development policy institutions; the education sector; and the research sector.

Financial management

New **budgetary reforms** have been carried out. Parliament approved the second part of the follow-up of the proposals by the Royal Commission on Organisational and Budgetary Reforms (1989). The first part of the reforms was implemented in 1990. The reforms aim towards budgeting for results and more efficient use of resources, giving more discretion to institutions in both financial and organisational matters, and enhancing accountability and improving result evaluation and control.

The modernisation of **"Public Property Management"** is included in these reforms. This modernisation encompasses, among other things, the introduction of rent payment by user institutions, more freedom of choice for user institutions, and the transformation of the Directorate of Public Construction and Property into a public enterprise.

Management of human resources

Personnel policies have been further developed within the framework of the overall public management reform strategy of the Ministry of Labour and Government Administration. Special attention is being paid to performance-oriented and result-oriented management by developing and implementing an employer policy with emphasis on well-qualified managers responsible for a satisfactory personnel policy, and by developing a set of regulations and agreements that will make result-oriented leadership possible.

After negotiations with the main unions, the Ministry implemented a new **pay system** for the civil service in May 1991. Important aspects of the new system are increased flexibility and more scope for the civil service to recruit and retain qualified personnel. Positions at the same level now have different salary alternatives, depending upon job situation, responsibility, competence and performance. Through these more dynamic pay policies, ministries and agencies will have a new tool for the management of human resources, and thus will be more able to achieve their main objectives.

Shortly after the implementation of the new pay system, 450 senior managers were excluded from "The Basic Collective Agreement". Their salaries and working conditions will instead be regulated by individual agreements. These agreements promote the possibilities of discussing and setting performance-related objectives, and of relating remuneration of senior managers to performance.

Supplementary reference material (all in Norwegian only)

NOU 1991:8 & Ot. prp. nr. 32 (1990-91) Lov om statsforetak (State-owned Enterprise Act). Ministry of Labour and Government Administration, Oslo, 1991.

NOU 1991:26 Om bruk av styrer i statlige virksomheter (Guidelines for the Use of Public Boards). Ministry of Labour and Government Administration, Oslo, 1991.

NOU 1991:28 Mot bedre vitende? Effektiviseringsmuligheter i offentlig sektor (Without Knowing Better? The Potential for Increased Cost-effectiveness in the Public Sector). Ministry of Labour and Government Administration, Oslo, 1991.

NOU 1991:5 & St. prp. nr. 63 (1990-91) Modernisering av den statlige eiendomsforvaltning (Modernisation of the Public Property Management). Ministry of Labour and Government Administration, Oslo, 1991.

St. prp. nr. 65 (1990-91) Om endringer i statens budsjettsystem (Changes in the Budget System). Ministry of Finance, Oslo, 1991.

NOU 1990:32 Statens lønnskomite av 1988 (The New Pay System). Ministry of Labour and Government Administration, Oslo, 1990.

FACTSHEET: NORWAY

A. PRINCIPAL RECENT PUBLIC MANAGEMENT DEVELOPMENTS

1986:
– New local authority income system introduced with greater use of lump-sum transfers from central to local government.
– Free municipality experiment starts to test impact of reducing central government regulations and transfering tasks from regional to local level.
– Positions of advisor and project manager created outside normal civil service hierarchy, in line with the policy of upward mobility.

1986/87:
– Changes to budgetary system give agencies more spending freedom and more accountability for results.

1987:
– New programme of public management improvement approved ("The New State"), providing a framework, guidelines and 75 specific measures.
– Royal Commission appointed to prepare basis for re-organisation and adaptation of managerial and control systems.

1988:
– Ministerial re-organisations aim to improve management.
– Committee appointed to propose new salary system for civil service with greater flexibility and scope for recruiting and retaining qualified staff.

1989:
– Royal Commission on Organisational and Budgetary Reforms proposes guidelines on organisational structures and forms, and recommends increased diversification within the government agency model, standardisation of state-owned enterprises and re-organisation of public enterprises. It also recommends budgetary reforms to increase efficiency and scope for political management.
– Expert group set up to start measuring productivity of public sector services and efficiency in public sector resource allocation.
– A Commission report on "Government IT Policies in the 1990s" emphasises integration, co-ordination and standardisation of IT throughout the administration.
– Launch of a bi-monthly newsletter reporting on modernisation projects.
– Overall responsibility for initiating, co-ordinating and monitoring public management reform given to new Ministry of Labour and Government Administration.
– Royal Commission appointed to examine ways of simplifying the structure of laws and reducing their number.
– Royal Commission appointed to evaluate the relationship between the geographical structure of municipalities/counties and the provision of public services, administration and local democracy.

1989-91:
– Reform programme for central government authorities at local level with the aim of improving efficiency, service quality, democracy and co-ordination.

1990:
– Three-year experiment to strengthen co-ordination role of county governors.
– Result-oriented financial management implemented and all ministries and agencies required to have corporate plan by end of year.
– Royal Commission appointed to develop a better organisational model for state-owned enterprises.
– Royal Commission appointed to examine simplification of laws relating to setting up a business.
– OMEGA project set up to develop task flow systems for the 1990s, primarily for the public administration.
– Royal Commission report proposes a new act relating to municipalities and counties. During 1992 the Government will present a proposition to Parliament on a new Local Government Act.
– Budgetary reforms implemented as first part of the follow-up of the report of the 1989 Royal Commission on Organisational and Budgetary Reforms.

1990-93:
– Government's Long-Term Programme advocates organisational, budgetary, regulatory, and managerial reform and wider introduction of IT.

B.   INSTITUTIONAL RESPONSIBILITY FOR PUBLIC MANAGEMENT IMPROVEMENT

ORGANISATION	TASKS AND RESPONSIBILITIES	OTHER INFORMATION
Ministry of Labour and Government Administration – Department of Management Policy and Administration – Department of Government Employer Affairs	– initiate, monitor and co-ordinate public management reforms – personnel policy, salaries	
Directorate of Public Management	– advice and assistance to the Government, ministries, and agencies on financial management, corporate planning, introduction of IT, management development, organisational development, service improvements, training and development	Independent agency reporting to the Ministry of Labour and Government Administration.
Ministry of Finance	– budgetary reforms	
Ministry of Local Government	– economic and legislative frames for counties and municipalities	

PORTUGAL

Important initiatives undertaken in 1991 by the **Secretariat for Administrative Modernisation** include:

- Publishing and enforcing Decree Law 129/91 dated 2 April 1991, which contains several measures to ease and simplify the relationship between the administration and users, including the reception of all citizens.
- A first seminar on new technologies and administrative modernisation.
- The publication of information guides on administrative activities, services available, and citizen rights (Commercial Trader Guide, House Buyers Guide, Reception Services Guide, etc.).
- The second National Day of Debureaucratisation, with important participation by public service representatives. Special reference was made to measures including:
  - launching EURO-SIMAPA (with EC information in the field of agriculture, fishing and food);
  - increasing the number of services available during the lunch hour;
  - opening reception and information services in some hospitals and special telephone lines for information in some of them;
  - adoption by some services of an automatic payment system;
  - simplification and free distribution of forms;
  - dissemination of information to the users of public services (lectures, leaflets, radio programmes, visits to public services);
  - increased decentralisation of social security and civil identification services; and
  - reduction of time to render services.
- Promotion of the Sectoral Modernisation Plans in all ministries.
- Approval of a new Government Programme which has as its main modernisation objectives to improve the quality of public services, to reinforce professional education and human resources management, and to re-organise public administration tasks in order to decentralise, regionalise, deconcentrate, and privatise.
- The decision by the new Government to subordinate all central services of public administration (National Institute of Administration (INA), Centre of Autarchic Studies, and Professional Instruction Department of Public Administration Management) to the **Secretariat for Administrative Modernisation.** This seeks to improve rationalisation of means, structures and equipment and to execute a global and integrated professional training programme.
- Evaluation of the programme concerning the public administration salary system.
- Launching of a "self-service" information system (INFOME) by the Education Ministry.
- Development of INFOCID (a system of information for citizens).
- Creation of scholarships and research studies for advanced training in public management.

In addition, the Administrative Procedure Code was published at the end of 1991, but is not yet in force.

Information systems and information technologies, and organisational changes

Main activities developed by the Institute of Informatics (II) within the global process of administrative modernisation include the INFOCID project, the INFOJUR project, and Public Accounting Reform.

INFOCID is a system of information for citizens which aims to give the public, either through specific reception services or directly, all information it needs about the public administration and the way it works. In other words, INFOCID is intended to allow citizens to obtain answers to questions about the entire public administration, such as: What to do? How to do it? Where to go?

On 2 May 1991, a decision from the Council of Ministers institutionalised the system, and on 20 June a public session was held to launch INFOCID, with the participation of all bodies involved in the project – namely, the Secretariat for Administrative Modernisation (the sponsoring body), the Secretariat of the Presidency of the Council of Ministers (the executive body), and the II (the host body) – as well as current and potential information producers. The structural and organisational pre-conditions for the development of the project were created in 1991. The system is expected to be fully operational in 1992.

The **INFOJUR project** aims to construct an integrated bank of juridical information by co-operating with several producers of normative documents. All normative documents published since 1980 in the First Series of the Official Journal (DR) are being loaded, together with some documents published before that date.

In addition to the legislation published in the DR (the main source of legislative information), in February 1991 the loading of sectoral information on work regulations (REGTRAB) was completed. This sectoral database has about 10 000 references on work regulations. REGTRAB is now fully operational with several inter-departmental connections.

Budget management and Public Accounting Reform is one of the most important structural reforms taking place in the Portuguese public administration. It is based on a profound change of principles and management methods, and it can be characterised in three areas: legislation, informatics system, and training. The informatics system is the strategic vector which will ease and regulate the change. The Public Accounting Department, through the II, will provide the three informatics systems covering the reforms needed:

- SIC: accounting information system;
- GRH: human resources management system;
- GP: property management system.

Together the three systems are called SIGO (Information System for Budget Management). The development of automation systems (II responsibility) reached its highest level in 1991. Availability to other parts of the public administration is expected at the beginning of 1992.

Together with the public accounting reform, the Treasury Department is also developing a reform of its own structures. One of the objectives is the simplification of payments. Computer resources for its realisation will be provided by the II.

During 1991, **two seminars were held** on information systems and information technologies (IS and IT) and their role in the organisational changes. The first, organised in May by the National Institute of Administration with the co-operation of II and SMA, had as its main objective to discuss the problematic of IS and the streamlining of public services from the perspective of top managers, who were the targeted participants.

The second seminar, organised by II with the support of INA and SMA, had the purposes of identifying the present conditions of IS and IT in the public administration, of discussing the need for a strategic approach to the development of IS and IT, and of identifying the conditions for the success of such an approach. This seminar was mainly addressed to those responsible for computer centres and services and/or the co-ordination of information policies in the public administration.

Both seminars led to a better understanding of the problems and of the need of approaching the subject of administrative modernisation through new perspectives – namely organisational information systems.

Financial management

The **Public Accounting Basic Law** was published in 1990. This law defines the principles and rules which must be obeyed by the financial services of central administration bodies and those institutes responsible for public funds. It also deals with budget control and the accounting of income and expenses. The law grants those services **administrative autonomy** in management actions by giving their directors the authority to approve expenses and their payment and to execute specified administrative actions. These do not include the fundamental activity options of the services and bodies.

Financial autonomy may be given to services which require it for their management and which have their own income covering at least two-thirds of total expenses. Services with financial autonomy have their own property and administrative autonomy.

Services with administrative autonomy are subject, *a posteriori,* to systematic budget control, including an inspection of legal compliance and the finance regularity of expenses. This also includes an analysis of **effectiveness and efficiency.** A budget management report of this control is presented to the minister responsible, and it can be the result of direct analysis of accounting data. Bodies with administrative autonomy will have a liability or responsibility account in addition to a cash account. Bodies with financial autonomy are also subject to systematic control of their budget management.

In 1991, the **General Budget Legislation** was published, establishing the principles and rules related to budget preparation, execution and control, as well as principles applicable to the State General Account. This law allows budget expenses to be presented by programmes, and provides for a more informative annex to the budget which permits better justification of budget policy. This law brought into the budget all income and expenses of the central administration including those related to autonomous services and funds with a new budget structure. It also defined the context of the State General Account which includes the accounts of all organisms of the central administration.

FACTSHEET: PORTUGAL

A. PRINCIPAL RECENT PUBLIC MANAGEMENT DEVELOPMENTS

1986:
- Secretariat for Administrative Modernisation (SMA) set up to guide reforms.

1987:
- Modernisation of the public administration established as a priority by the Government with over-riding goal of gradually reducing the role of the State in the economy.
- Commission for Enterprise/Administration Relationships (CEAR) created and attached to the SMA.

1988:
- Law passed allowing conversion of public companies into enterprises with capital shared between public and private sectors.
- CEAR sets up seven project teams as part of an inter-ministerial programme for debureaucratisation.

1989:
- Revision of Portuguese Constitution leading to new Law of Principles on privatisation guaranteeing transparency of privatisation process.
- Reforms to civil service pay system to improve client service and staff motivation by improving internal consistency and transparency and external competitiveness.
- Public Accounting Reform initiative launched by Ministry of Finance to increase administrative autonomy of line departments, establish a system of *a posteriori* budget controls and improve management in the central administration.
- Government decision to measure the efficiency of agencies and a Management Audit Team set up, directly responsible to the Minister of Finance.

1990:
- Reforms to the Court of Auditors to strengthen its independence, simplify the decision-making process, increase the number of bodies reporting to it and decentralise its activities.
- National Day for Debureaucratisation established to promote new initiatives.
- New law launches major new reprivatisation programme.
- New Code of Administrative Procedures approved to simplify relations between the administration and citizens and to reduce regulatory obligations.
- Computerised local area network set up to link cabinets of members of Government with the aim of reducing paper flows and enhancing the information system.

B. INSTITUTIONAL RESPONSIBILITY FOR PUBLIC MANAGEMENT IMPROVEMENT

ORGANISATION	TASKS AND RESPONSIBILITIES	OTHER INFORMATION
Secretariat for Administrative Modernisation (SMA)	– guide modernisation measures, particularly by simplifying bureaucratic procedures – implement a new civil service pay system and introduce flexibility in manpower management	Established in 1986; headed by the Secretary of State for Administrative Modernisation, who is directly responsible to the Prime Minister.
Centre of Technical Studies and Legislative Support (CETAL)	– management of regulatory reform	Reports to the Presidency of the Council of Ministers.
Ministry of Finance	– budgetary reform	
– General Directorate for Public Administration	– human resources management and organisational adjustment – permanent staff inspection system	
– Institute of Informatics	– introduction and use of information technology	
Court of Auditors	– control of public expenditures	Independent tribunal.

SPAIN

Re-organisation of ministries

The reshaping of the Government in March 1991 was accompanied by substantial restructuring in a number of ministries, with two basic aims: adjusting the central government to meet one of its most important challenges, the **Single European Market** of 1993, and progressively introducing the **modernisation measures** advocated by the Ministry of Public Administration.

The number of ministries was cut from 17 to 16, by merging public works and town planning with transport in a Ministry of Public Works and Transport which is now responsible for virtually all central government spending on non-military infrastructure and facilities. The Ministry of Industry was enlarged with trade (an area removed from the Ministry of the Economy and Finance) and tourism, which had previously come under the Ministry of Transport. There was also substantial re-organisation inside ministries whose general range of responsibilities was unchanged; these included the Ministries of Agriculture, Fisheries and Food and of Health and Consumer Affairs.

On the **modernisation** side, all the restructuring was designed to form ministries covering homogeneous and differentiated areas of activity (modules or departments), allowing scope for more autonomous management subject to the political control of the minister. These areas are headed by a State Secretary or Secretary-General, to whom the General Directors report.

Management of human resources

The development, and introduction in 1992, of a methodology for medium and long-term planning of human resources is designed to increase managers' involvement in determining staffing requirements, to co-ordinate the various stages of the process, and to make selection procedures more flexible.

There has been an amendment of the **selection procedures** for entry to the public service, in line with the concern to adjust tests and examinations to the requirements of the post to be filled. Emphasis on memorisation and theoretical knowledge has been reduced, and greater weight has been given to criteria such as experience, occupational career, etc.

Analysis has been made of services having the greatest **impact on citizens,** to review improvements and remaining problem areas, and to set indicators for service quality in mail delivery, education, health, employment, social services and social security, and documentation.

Extension of modernisation schemes

To secure political backing at the highest executive level, the Minister for Public Administration proposed that the Government enter into an agreement to develop a plan for the modernisation of the State administration. The **Government Agreement** was approved in November 1991. It sets a number of guidelines and targets for improvements and binds all ministries to develop specific schemes under the direction and control of two committees, one chaired by the Vice-President of the Government and the other by the Minister for Public Administration.

The aims of the agreement are:

- to modernise the administration and improve public services;
- to link the staff representation and collective bargaining processes; and

- to improve working conditions for public employees, upgrading their occupational skills and enhancing their profile.

These in turn will be embodied in projects along the following lines:

- improving information for citizens and citizen-administration communications, making full use of information technology;
- improving substantive aspects of specified public services; and
- developing overall efforts to modernise specific units or agencies, incorporating improvements in external management.

The Ministry of Public Administration will have a major role to play in co-ordinating the process and providing technical support for other ministries.

The Government Agreement was supplemented by a further agreement signed the same month with the trade unions represented in the public service to modernise the administration and improve working conditions. This covers 1992, 1993 and 1994. The purpose is not simply to achieve a conflict-free atmosphere needed to tackle the modernisation of the public service effectively, but to **involve staff actively** in the process as well. The topics covered give an idea of the agreement's scope: drafting of job descriptions, promotion and training, public employment, re-organisation and restructuring, working hours and the working week, social measures, assistance to families, and health and safety.

Supplementary funds were also established to improve **remuneration.** They will be linked in part to specific modernisation projects, among those set down in the Government Agreement. There are also provisions regarding arrangements for **collective bargaining** in the future, designed to schedule it at set periods, partly devolve it in some sectors and departments, and promote satisfactory procedures for dispute settlement.

Other modernisation measures

The Spanish Airports and Air Navigation Agency started operation, after becoming a public body with substantial management autonomy. Its staff is now subject to general labour law rather than being public employees, as was previously the case.

As a result of a parliamentary initiative, a committee of experts was set up to study the **national health system** and its current and future development. The committee's non-binding report (the Abril report) was published in July 1991. The most notable recommendations concerning the organisation and operation of the network of public health institutions are:

- to promote greater responsibility among the system's managers for more effective use of resources within a more autonomous framework; and
- to create structures capable of adjusting expenditure flexibly and autonomously to budget appropriations.

Impetus has been given to **information technology,** to developing new software applications for administrative management, and to proposing quality indicators for services. The second national IT workshop (TECNIMAP, December 1991) was attended by representatives of central government, the Autonomous Communities, and local authorities.

FACTSHEET: SPAIN

A. PRINCIPAL RECENT PUBLIC MANAGEMENT DEVELOPMENTS

1985:
- Multi-lateral co-operative commissions set up as co-ordination mechanism between central and regional bodies.
- National Commission for Local Administration created to strengthen co-operation between central and local authorities.

1987:
- "Operative Service Inspections" method introduced as a tool to rationalise administrative management.

1988:
- Ministry of the Government Spokesman established to co-ordinate the information services of the central administration.
- Ministry of Social Affairs established to co-ordinate execution of the Government's policy on social services, and to encourage conditions allowing for social equality of the sexes and more participation by women in political, cultural, economic and social life.
- New law on local finance provides for a funding system with simplified local taxation, and with restructured budget procedures. This law is based on principles of autonomy with shared responsibilities.

1988/89:
- Principle of co-operation between government agencies applied in agreements between central, regional and local levels of administration (150 signed between central and regional authorities in 1988, some 200 in 1989).

1989:
- Ministry of Public Administration (MPA) prepares a basic discussion document "Reflections on Modernisation of the Public Administration" to seek consensus on guidelines, strengthen philosophy of a public service culture considering citizens as clients, progressively incorporate management by objectives and promote decentralised management.
- "Administrative module" concept introduced as basic organisational unit for facilitating effective management.
- Use of competitive entrance examinations for civil servants extended to cover about 90 per cent of all posts involved.
- Survey of public managers' evaluation of modernisation proposals.
- Inter-ministerial committee of experts on human resource management (CORHAP) set up.
- Working group created to make recommendations for action on administrative organisation and procedures.

1989/90:
- Presentation and discussion of MPA document with politicians, senior civil servants and representatives of other interested groups.
- Co-operation between central government and Autonomous Communities in form of signed agreements (250 each year) and bilateral or multilateral commissions.
- Introduction of numerous measures designed to make human resources management more forward-looking (e.g. registers of posts).
- Higher Information Processing Council empowered to undertake range of projects on the role of IT in the modernisation process.

1990:
- Publication of an "Administrative Language Style Manual".
- Decentralised personnel policy introduced transferring many powers to managers.
- An "integral plan for information for citizens" drawn up.
- Ministry of the Economy and Finance establishes mechanisms to simplify control procedures.
- Creation of new IT units aimed at eliminating shortage of professional IT staff in central administration.

1990/91:
- Changes to the legal status of bodies such as the Spanish Tourism Institute, State Tax Agency, and Post and Telegraph Agency.
- Intensification and decentralisation of training efforts: National Institute for Public Administration strengthened and made responsible for drawing up a management training plan.

B. INSTITUTIONAL RESPONSIBILITY FOR PUBLIC MANAGEMENT IMPROVEMENT

ORGANISATION	TASKS AND RESPONSIBILITIES	OTHER INFORMATION
Ministry of Public Administration	– promotion of the modernisation of public administration – improvement of citizen-administration relations	
Ministry of the Economy and Finance	– prepares the State budget – controls public expenditure, including salaries of public servants	

SWEDEN

As a result of the general elections in September 1991, Sweden now has a centre-right four-party coalition Government in power. This Government – under a Conservative Prime Minister and a Liberal Minister of Finance – has set as one of its political goals to change the economy from a traditional "Swedish model" economy into a more market-oriented one. That means – both in the short run and in the long run – a change in public sector activities, leading also to changes in public management.

Making the public sector more efficient

A build-up during the post-war period has made the public sector an essential component of the Swedish economic system. The public sector in Sweden is large compared to other OECD Member countries and the distribution of welfare is more widespread and uniform than in most other countries, due in large measure to the public service system.

Towards the end of the 1980s, the size of the public sector turned out to be a serious problem for the Swedish economy and consequently for welfare. At a time of general economic recession, it became more and more obvious that the stagnation of the efficiency of the public sector threatened the country's whole economy. The new economic policy therefore includes efforts to renew and limit the public sector.

The Administrative Reform Programme

An important provision for the new Government's aim of restricting public expenditure is a long-term strategy of expenditure. Parliament has endorsed the concept of a long-term strategy for public expenditure. Such a strategy requires:

- an assessment of the **long-term** development of expenditure;
- a frame for **total expenditure,** with breakdown over time as well as by political priorities. The total expenditure frame must be determined so as to meet the requirements for desired economic development in the longer run; and
- **annual controls** to determine the expenditure frame for a new three-year period.

Improved public management is to be achieved by setting targets, clearly specifying the required results, and analysing and evaluating the results thus achieved. **Management by results** is fundamental to the budgetary process. The managerial perspective is to be broadened, however, with greater emphasis on **analyses and evaluations** of a multi-sectoral nature. The intention is that the Government should ensure such analyses on a continuous basis. Methodological competence will be enhanced in the Government Chancery (the small Swedish ministries) as well as at the broad agency level. The governmental decision-making process will also be adapted to the requirements for achieving objectives of budget policy and the long-term expenditure strategy. This should be done by introducing frame budgeting into the Government Chancery.

An issue which must be considered before deciding on the management of any activity is whether the activity is a matter for the Government or not. The Government has presented a strategy for management of the remaining activities of the Government agencies.

The forms in which national public activities should be undertaken will be clarified. The work of **delegating responsibilities and authority** to the agencies will continue. This pre-supposes a clear system of rules which spell out the discretionary authority of the agencies.

Conditions will be created for **rational decision-making** by the agencies. Increased delegation also demands a great deal in the way of agency accounting, as well as efficient auditing. It will be necessary, finally, to clarify the responsibilities of their directors-general and boards.

The following points describe the strategy in more detail:

– Activities open to competition should not, under normal circumstances, be undertaken by the Government.
– Competitive activities carried out at present by the agencies will therefore be re-assessed.
– Management by results in the central administration is to be developed, and to be accompanied by increased requirements. Governmental assessments of the activities will focus on agency accounts and results.
– Requirements are to be tightened as regards agency accounts and competence in economic administration. The financial authority of agencies should be linked to economic performance. A system of agency ratings should be drawn up.
– The management of activities financed through fees should be a separate entity.
– A model comprising frames for administrative costs of agencies is presented with a view to giving agencies a clearer responsibility for costs.
– A system should be constructed so as to yield interest on the funds at the disposal of agencies. This would promote cost consciousness and efficient cash management.
– Appropriations for administrative investments are to be replaced in stages by agency borrowing from the National Debt Office.
– Guidelines are presented for the implementation of leasing in the central administration.
– Agencies are authorised to make decisions about their premises.
– Proposals are submitted to revoke the monopoly of the Postal Giro for handling central government payments.

Further details are given in Annex 1 of the Government's 1992 Budget Bill, which is to be decided upon by the Parliament in May 1992, covering the budgetary year 1 July 1992 to 30 June 1993.

Development of the working methods of the Government and its Chancery

The new Government has re-organised its Chancery, as of 1 December 1991. Through this re-organisation, central matters of public administration are now handled by the Ministry of Finance, while the Ministry of Public Administration is still responsible for regional and local administration, as well as community development and consumer protection. Competition matters are taken care of by a reinforced Ministry of Industry and Commerce. The Ministry of Housing and Physical Planning has been abolished through deregulation in this area, and a new Ministry of Culture has been established for matters of culture, immigration and equality between the sexes.

Last but not least, the Cabinet Office (Prime Minister's Office) has been reinforced with a political Co-ordination Chancery; while, as of 1 March 1992, some judicial co-ordination responsibilities will be left to the Ministry of Justice.

The transition to a more systematic budgetary analysis and long-term expenditure strategy and the change-over to a budgetary framework – together with world-wide changes – call for an investigation of the Chancery's organisation and working methods. A special investigator is to be appointed.

Demand and competition

The new coalition Government would like to introduce an extended use of market mechanisms instead of regulations in the offer/demand relation of public service. It also makes a strong point of privatising public services.

Adapting the national administration to an open Europe

Internationalisation may require measures to achieve greater economy in some fields and, in others, additional resources. The re-adjustment of the national administration is therefore to proceed in such a way that opportunities for reaping administrative benefits can be acted upon, at the same time as the integration process can be conducted in keeping with the Parliament's intentions. During the spring of 1991, an enquiry was made to consider measures whereby Sweden's administration could be suitably equipped for its tasks in the future process of integration. Measures based on the enquiry are to be presented to the Parliament in 1992.

Human resource management connected with structural changes

Necessary structural rationalisation measures in the national administration are made feasible by a **comprehensive and advanced job security system,** which came into force on 1 April 1991. This system covers all employees within the Government agencies and other agencies for which the National Agency for Government Employers (SAV) negotiates. Its function is to prevent unemployment in the event of work scarcity and relocation of the place of work. This is carried out in three ways: preventive measures for continued employment; support in finding a new job; help when a person finds himself or herself unemployed.

The system is based on an agreement between the Government and the relevant central trade unions. In accordance with the agreement, a Job Security Foundation has been established. The Foundation's work is financed by money agreed upon in the collective salary negotiations. At the end of 1991, the Foundation had a capital of approximately SKr 475 million.

Salaries and pensions

The flexible system of wages and salaries introduced in 1989 is now in full operation. However, there has not yet been any evaluation of its effect.

In order to keep inflation low, SAV and the unions have come to a collective agreement (RALS 1991-93) for the period 1 January 1991 to 31 March 1993 with very low salary increases. The agreement is based upon proposals from a Government Commission (the Rehnberg group). According to the agreement, salaries have increased from 1 January 1991 by 1.15 per cent (non-level-increasing). From 1 July 1991, there were small increases (maximum of SKr 209 per month for employees earning no more than SKr 14 200 per month). From 1 April 1992, the salaries may increase by a maximum of 3 per cent; wage drift will lower the percentage. Similar agreements have been made for almost the entire Swedish labour market.

A new pension scheme for civil servants will come into effect on 1 January 1992. The new scheme is similar to those in the private sector. In principle, it has the same retirement age for all employees (age 65). According to the new pension scheme, 1.55 per cent of each employee's annual salary is set aside for an additional pension.

New measures taken in the negotiating work

During 1991, further steps were taken to reinforce the line of **decentralisation** in implementing employer's policy and collective agreements within the government sector.

- When the agreements on the compensation connected with travelling expenses on duty had to be renegotiated in consequence of a tax reform, new agreements were worked out for each agency, not for the civil service as a whole.
- Classification by a position system has been agreed upon and has been introduced. This system is to form the basis for the wage and salary statistics in the civil service and is intended to serve as a support for the agencies in their individual setting of payments. Most important, the classification system is comparable to and partly equivalent to the corresponding system used within the private sector.

Fewer and simpler rules

For several years, extensive work has been in progress to simplify the rules governing public activities as well as private ones. The latest report on this subject was given in Annex 2 of the Budget Bill 1991.

The regulatory reform work continues, especially in order to speed up **deregulation** and thereby achieve better effectiveness and possibilities of privatisation. Resource-consuming regulatory systems are scrutinised to investigate the possibilities of re-appraisal and simplification. Two examples can be cited: in the field of social insurance, regulatory reforms (such as the introduction of an employer's liability period for sickness allowance) are to bring about active rehabilitation; a new policy for the production and consumption of food implies the dismantling of internal market regulations.

Management of regulatory review and reform

The impact of computerised data bases on regulatory review continues to reduce the number of laws and ordinances in force in Sweden. The agencies' regulations also continue to diminish in number. Between 1990 and 1991, more than 1 000 such regulations were abolished (according to statistics dated 1 September 1991). For instance, about 60 per cent of the number of administrative rules issued by the 24 county administrative boards are no longer in force.

Strengthening the local level of government

The transition to **management by results** also implies new demands on regional and local authorities. For example: management and resource utilisation in the higher education sector are now under review; and responsibility for the administration of personnel and finance within the courts of justice and the public prosecution authorities should be transferred to the regional or local level.

A **freer hand** has been given to **municipalities** (communes) through the abolition of detailed regulations, thus improving the ability of municipalities to adapt their activities to the demands of the public. This policy is said to be continued by the new Government.

The **Local Government Act of 1991,** governing the activities of Sweden's municipalities and county councils with effect from 1 January 1992, gives them extensive liberty to design and modify their own organisational structure in keeping with local conditions.

Due to the low rate of economic growth and the necessity of avoiding tax increases, the needs of the general public can no longer be met by means of additional funding. **Re-appraisal, rationalisa-**

tion and **efficiency improvement** are becomming necessary ingredients of all municipal and county council activities. A process can be discerned whereby local government activities are becoming increasingly characterised by deregulation and market orientation.

The new Local Government Act stands for **deregulation.** In addition, the Government has declared its intention of presenting a bill introducing a new **funding system,** in which earmarked grants will be replaced by single, general allocation. It will be the responsibility of Parliament to define national goals for the activities of local authorities, giving the latter extensive liberty to choose their own ways of achieving those goals.

Under the present Government, there is a strong trend to favour **privatisation** and to dissolve existing public monopolies in the local government sector. This trend has already expressed itself by encouraging, for example, child-care centres and kindergartens run by parents, by the employees or by private firms. Another example would be publicly-owned libraries run by private entrepreneurs.

Municipalities and county councils are thus making efforts to cope with the current economic situation by stressing the element of **market orientation** in their activities. In certain municipalities, efforts are being made to reduce activities to a ''client-performer'' model. This model consistently distinguishes between the roles of elected politicians as consumer representatives on one hand and responsible producers on the other.

Development is also in progress whereby municipal activities are being exposed to an increasing measure of **competition** along two lines: increased competition between public sector activities and private contractors; and increased competition within the framework of public sector activities. There is also a tendency for municipalities and county councils to form limited companies for the conduct of operations, especially in the technical sector.

FACTSHEET: SWEDEN

A.   PRINCIPAL RECENT PUBLIC MANAGEMENT DEVELOPMENTS

1981:   – Independent Expert Group on Public Finance (ESO) set up by the Ministry of Finance to carry out studies of central and local government including monetary transfers within the welfare state system and measuring the productivity of agencies.

1985:   – Experiment initiated in three-year budget frames for all administrative expenditures.

1987:   – A Parliamentary Decision on Public Management and a Government Agency Ordinance set guidelines for administrative reform and require agencies to improve access to public services.

1988/89:   – New instructions for 200 agencies introduce decentralisation process, focus on results and long-term objectives, and increased autonomy and discretionary authority for agency managers.

1989:   – Government presents guidelines for public sector renewal in a Supplementary Budget Bill.
                 – Re-organisation and re-inforcement of Ministry of Public Administration emphasises its role as leader of renewal process and the importance of results and their measurement.
                 – More flexible system of wages and salaries introduced and the Public Employment Act modernised.
                 – More flexibility introduced into recruitment and mobility of senior executives; study launched on their remuneration and pay scales.
                 – Special government ordinance on budgetary reform put into effect concerning three-year budget frames.
                 – Methodology for determining the costs of regulations refined.

1989-91:   – "Free municipality experiment" in increasing the autonomy of local authorities sets aside uniform national legislation/regulations and aims to restructure central, regional and municipal relations.

1990:   – Ongoing re-organisation of budget process gives greater attention to specifying results.
                 – Government announces a programme to re-adjust and slim down the national administration by 10 per cent over three years based on decentralisation, deregulation and internationalisation.
                 – Number of laws and ordinances in force at lowest level for at least 20 years as a result of regulatory review and computerisation.
                 – Expanded survey of regulatory impact.

1990/91:   – New Local Government Act concludes a comprehensive process of reform reflecting rapid changes in local government during the 1980s and includes provisions for clearer local government powers, financial management reforms, giving more importance to accounting and auditing, and freer committee structures.

B. INSTITUTIONAL RESPONSIBILITY FOR PUBLIC MANAGEMENT IMPROVEMENT

ORGANISATION	TASKS AND RESPONSIBILITIES	OTHER INFORMATION
Ministry of Finance	– budgetary reform, budget development, personnel policy, pay, pensions – overall responsibility and co-ordination of public management reforms	An independent Expert Group on Public Finance (ESO) conducts studies related to budgetary and economic policy-making (e.g. productivity and effectiveness in the public sector).
– Swedish Agency for Administrative Development (SAFAD)	– implementation of public management reforms at agency level	
– National Agency for Government Employers (SAV)	– implementation of new personnel policy	
– National Audit Bureau (RRV)	– development of methods regarding result-based management	
– National Institute for Civil Service Training and Development (SIPU)	– promotion of efficiency, competence and quality in the public sector through training programmes, consulting services, publications, seminars, and special studies	
Ministry of Public Administration	– regional and local administration, community development, consumer protection	
Ministry of Industry and Commerce	– regulatory reviews and reforms with reference to rules concerning trade and industry	
Cabinet Office (i.e. Prime Minister's Office)	– overall co-ordination of government policy	

SWITZERLAND

Organisational and structural change, and financial management

Following an initial series of pilot projects, the Federal Council decided on 16 January 1991 to continue the introduction of "**management control**", which is both a method and philosophy of management, into the federal administration. It approved a second series of projects which are both more complex (management in agriculture, research and higher education institutions, and management in connection with the implementation of the Act on investment in mountain regions) and of a new type (management information systems for the Federal Railways and the Post and Telecommunications). Subsequently, a managent control project concerning the Directorate for Development Co-operation and Humanitarian Aid was launched.

By the end of 1991 the feasibility studies for these projects had been completed. The results were positive. They showed that management control can be applied successfully to large-scale strategic and operational activities in the public sector. At the same time, in response to a growing interest in management control, a big effort was made to provide information and training via numerous meetings and seminars, both in Switzerland and abroad.

Management of human resources

With regard to **performance-related pay,** on 1 May 1991 the Federal Council implemented Section 45 (2a) of the Act on the conditions of service of civil servants, which states: "In making real increases in the amounts indicated in Section 36 and in granting ordinary or exceptional increases in pay under Sections 40 and 41, due account will be taken of the performance of the civil servant." In this connection, it should be noted that the "Instructions concerning the elements determining remuneration", which were drawn up by the Federal Personnel Office, state that a civil servant should not receive an ordinary increase in real pay if it is established that he or she has not performed his or her duties satisfactorily.

In addition to Section 45 (2a) of the above-mentioned Act, government departments have another means of promoting individual effort. Within the framework of personnel rating, they can reward work that is deemed to be exceptional. The budget appropriation for such rewards has to be fixed every year; however, for budgetary reasons this measure has still not been implemented.

As regards **training,** the Federal Council plans to step up vocational training. Pilot schemes for the temporary exchange of personnel and for the introduction of flexible working hours are to be launched during the legislative period 1992-95.

Evaluation

The working party on legislative evaluation set up by the Federal Council in autumn 1987 completed its work recently. It looked closely at the advantages and disadvantages of legislative evaluation and put forward concrete proposals on ways of improving *ex post* and *ex ante* evaluation of government measures. Its proposals will be incorporated in the legislative guidelines for 1992-95.

FACTSHEET: SWITZERLAND

A.   PRINCIPAL RECENT PUBLIC MANAGEMENT DEVELOPMENTS

1980-84:   – The Federal Council submits to Parliament modifications to the Constitution and to legislation concerning the separation of responsibilities between the Confederation and the cantons.

1983:   – Review of tasks undertaken by departments under the responsibility of the Federal Chancellery aimed at reducing tasks not of high priority.

1984-87:   – Project on Increasing the Efficiency of the Federal Administration (EFFI) aimed at saving a total of 3 per cent of jobs, and 5 per cent of working time and general expenditure over three years.

1986:   – Establishment of a 42-hour working week as a result of EFFI with a significant reduction of administrative costs.

1986-90:   – Project on inter- and extra-departmental efficiency measures undertaken by a public sector firm, as an extension of the EFFI project, with a focus on 20 sectoral programmes (EFFI/Interdepartmental Measures).

1987:   – Creation of a working group on "legislative evaluation". Its tasks include making proposals to improve forecasts of the effects of legislation and to improve the control of the effectiveness of standards, and deciding how to implement those proposals.

1989:   – Federal Department of Finance launches study on management control to explore its contribution to efficiency and effectiveness, objective setting and political and financial management.

1990:   – Federal Office of Organisation replaced by a Federal Office of Information Technology (established under the auspices of the Federal Department of Finance to co-ordinate policies in IT) and its other tasks divided between the Federal Chancellery and Federal Office of Personnel.
     – System for monitoring the administration set up and a parliamentary body for "control" created on the initiative of the Management Commissions and a decision of the Federal Council.
     – Revision of the Act on the Organisation of the Administration gives wider mandate to the General Secretariat.
     – Four pilot projects set up as part of the management control initiative and first findings reported.

1991:   – The Federal Council decides to introduce management control on a large scale throughout the federal administration and to set up a new series of pilot projects. Three management control projects enter the implementation phase. Seven additional feasibility studies show that the goals of management control (set in 1989) can be progressively achieved.
     – The Federal Office of Personnel publishes "Instructions concerning the elements determining remuneration".
     – Working group develops proposals for the improvement of government.
     – Work begun under the National Research Programme No. 27, "Impact of State Measures".
     – Submission of final report of the working group on "legislative evaluation" containing proposals to improve retrospective and future evaluation of state measures.

B. INSTITUTIONAL RESPONSIBILITY FOR PUBLIC MANAGEMENT IMPROVEMENT

ORGANISATION	TASKS AND RESPONSIBILITIES	OTHER INFORMATION
Federal Chancellery – Administrative Control Service	– oversight of projects on increasing the efficiency of the Federal administration	
Federal Department of Finance – Federal Office of Personnel	– budget process – recruiting and maintaining appropriate federal personnel – negotiations with unions	
– Federal Office of Information Technology	– co-ordination of IT policies	A new unit established in 1990 to replace the Federal Office of Organisation where IT functions were previously situated.
Federal Department of Justice and Police – Federal Office of Justice	– assists in legislation	Also assists in the area of legislative methods.

TURKEY

Studies for cutting red tape and reducing bureaucratic formalities within the framework of public management development have been made by the Turkish Government, especially on the subject of licences, passports and registration issues. The total number of measures and improvements has exceeded 1 107 so far. Some of the important improvements completed in 1991 are described below.

The second volume of the booklet on **"Reducing Bureaucracy in Public Administration"** was published; it details initiatives taken since the publishing of the first volume in 1989. The booklet, which covers the period 1989/90, contains 635 initiatives to simplify procedures and to encourage other similar efforts.

Civil servants who lose their identification cards can now receive a new one from their institutions without having to apply to the police office.

The articles of the legislation related to the authorities and responsibilities of **village administrators** and administrative bodies were codified, and the booklets were distributed to villages all over the country.

In order to **modernise communication** and the flow of information and documents between public agencies, a standardised coding system has been developed using information technology. This system will go into effect on 1 January 1992.

Registration of blood groups on **driving licences** has been made obligatory, with the intention of facilitating first aid in the event of traffic accidents. At the request of the individual, information can also be registered on driving licences in order to facilitate organ donation. New technical methods have been adopted for detection of levels of alcohol following traffic accidents, thus reducing loss of time and effort.

The obligation of filling in **statistical forms** at the border when entering or leaving the country, for both Turkish citizens and foreigners, has been abolished. Passports of Turkish citizens who work and reside abroad will no longer be stamped at the Turkish borders, except for those who have not yet performed their military service and those citizens who deal with imports. Thus these citizens will not lose any rights which may arise from the legislation of the countries where they live and work.

Turkish companies which have contracts with the government will now be able to get their payments more easily and promptly by means of a "letter of credit" system which is being implemented.

FACTSHEET: TURKEY

A. PRINCIPAL RECENT PUBLIC MANAGEMENT DEVELOPMENTS

1983:
   – New economic policy introduced with policies on improving the efficiency and effectiveness of public management and a programme for structural adjustment.

1987:
   – Responsibility for improving the functioning of the public administration centralised by creation of the Directorate of Administrative Development in the Prime Minister's Office.
   – Measures introduced to eliminate excessive red-tape and to reduce the administrative burden of government procedures.
   – Structure of government machinery simplified by reducing the number of ministries from 35 to 21, cutting the number of hierarchical levels in the administration by half, and redefining the responsibilities of different levels.

1988:
   – Decentralisation and deconcentration programmes introduced in several sectors and a two-tier metropolitan system of government introduced in the largest cities.
   – Studies and new legislation to simplify the formalities for establishing small and medium-scale enterprises.

1989:
   – New project launched to create special units for improving relations with the public in all agencies with the aim of more effective and efficient service delivery and to develop strategy for informing citizens about government structures and functions.
   – Directorate of Administrative Development publishes booklet on "Reducing Bureaucracy in Public Administration" detailing initiatives taken since 1984 to simplify procedures and encouraging other similar efforts.
   – More objective criteria introduced for evaluating the performance of public servants, and incentives and an award system adopted.
   – In-service training opportunities increasingly offered to public servants of all levels along with analysis of the number and qualification requirements of new posts.

1990:
   – Numerous measures introduced to simplify regulations and procedures aimed at greater efficiency through savings of time for both staff and citizens.
   – Training activities, especially for staff in direct contact with the public, intensified and put onto an annual basis, under the auspices of the Prime Minister's Office.
   – More systematic application of IT in the administration leading to improved flow of documents and of information between public agencies.

B. INSTITUTIONAL RESPONSIBILITY FOR PUBLIC MANAGEMENT IMPROVEMENT

ORGANISATION	TASKS AND RESPONSIBILITIES	OTHER INFORMATION
Directorate of Administrative Development	– improvement of the functioning of the administrative machinery – reduction of red tape – initiation and co-ordination of reforms – monitoring implementation of initiatives introduced by other agencies	Reports directly to the Undersecretary of the Prime Ministry.
Ministry of Finance – Directorate General of Budgeting and Financial Control	– budgetary aspects of management reform	
State Personnel Department	– personnel management aspects of management reform	Agency reporting to the Prime Minister through a Minister of State.

UNITED KINGDOM

Next Steps: organisational and structural change in the civil service

By the end of 1991, after "Next Steps" (see page 113 of the 1990 Survey) had been operating for three and a half years, 57 Agencies were established, employing over 200 000 staff. The Agencies cover a wide range of organisations dealing with activities as diverse as weather forecasting, issuing driving licences, giving help to unemployed people, providing support to the armed forces and running government research establishments. The largest, the Social Security Benefits Agency which administers the delivery of social security benefits, has 66 000 staff; and the smallest, Wilton Park Conference Centre which runs conferences on international affairs, has 30. In addition to these 57 Agencies, Customs and Excise have 30 Executive Units with 27 000 staff operating along "Next Steps" lines and, by April 1992, the Inland Revenue will have established 34 Executive Offices employing over 60 000 staff. A further 32 potential Agency candidates, with over 33 000 staff, have been announced. It is expected that by April 1992, half the United Kingdom Civil Service will be operating fully along "Next Steps" lines and that there will be 70 Agencies by mid-1992.

The second review of "Next Steps" Agencies was published in November 1991 (HMSO Cm 1760) and contains many examples of what is being achieved.

Since the **Government Trading Funds Act 1990** (see page 114 of the 1990 Survey) came into operation, five new trading funds have been set up, making a total of seven. A number of other Agencies are working towards trading fund status.

In May 1991, the Prime Minister's Efficiency Unit published a report of a study carried out on the relationship between departments and Agencies (**"Making the Most of Next Steps"**). The report recommended that chief executives should be given greater authority and freedom in managing their Agencies, including the ability to shop around for support services. The "Next Steps" Project Manager is working with the Treasury and departments to take forward the ideas in the report.

Better quality service delivery

The **Citizen's Charter** was published in July 1991. The Charter is a set of initiatives "to make public services answer better to the wishes of their users and to raise their quality overall". It is reinforced by more detailed charters for individual services such as for patients, parents, jobseekers, and tenants.

The themes of the Charter are **quality, choice, standards,** and **value for money within the nation's tax bill.** It sets out a range of mechanisms and ideas which are designed to help improve the quality of public service in a variety of ways:

– more privatisation;
– wider competition and more contracting out;
– more performance-related pay;
– published performance targets and more information about standards;
– more effective complaints procedures and tougher, more independent inspectorates; and
– better redress for people when services go wrong.

Measures already announced include guaranteed maximum waiting times for certain National Health Service (NHS) treatments, fixed appointments for hospital out-patients, publication of league tables for schools' results, and new powers to protect the consumer. In a subsequent White Paper

("**Competing for Quality**"), the Government describes steps to make it easier for the private sector to compete in providing services to central government, local authorities, and the NHS.

"Next Steps", with its emphasis on improving management in government, has laid the foundations for the effective implementation of the Charter's aims. The Government has already announced that all Agencies will fully comply with the principles of the Charter.

Privatisation

Under the Government's privatisation programme, 46 major businesses have been privatised so far. Work is in hand on the privatisation of Northern Ireland Electricity, British Coal, and British Rail. Over 900 000 jobs have been transferred to the private sector, and the State-owned sector has been reduced by around two-thirds. Where privatisation is not appropriate, there has been an ongoing programme of reviews which aimed to open up public services to market pressures and disciplines through market testing and contracting out.

Management of human resources

The Government is in the process of renegotiating most **civil service pay agreements** (see page 114 of the 1990 Survey) in two main ways. First, the intention is to provide a more direct and regular link between individuals' pay and their performance. Second, the proposals would allow departments and Agencies to establish their own pay and grading system where this provided better value for money; and those departments and Agencies which remain within the central system would have scope for varying the distribution of the annual pay settlement.

Although the most senior grades (1 to 3) who make up the senior open structure are not covered by such agreements, the pay of Grades 2 and 3 are wholly related to performance under new arrangements which came into effect in April 1991. Eleven Agencies have negotiated **bonus pay schemes** and nine of these are in operation. Others have schemes under consideration. Bonuses are funded from cash released through efficiency savings.

In April 1991, departments and Agencies were given the **delegated authority** to recruit directly staff to junior and middle management grades (they already had authority to recruit clerical staff). Prior to that, recruitment to those posts had been carried out centrally by the Civil Service Commission. More generally, line managers are increasingly being given responsibility for staff development and other functions previously carried out by personnel branches and/or central departments.

Departments and Agencies are continuing to implement the civil service programme for action to achieve **equality of opportunity** for women. Four progress reports have now been published since its launch. To keep up the momentum, a new programme for action is to be launched in 1992. A good start has been made in implementing the programme for action to achieve equality of opportunity for people of ethnic minority origin, introduced in May 1990. A report on progress in the first year was published in December 1991.

Financial management

Proposals in the White Paper "Competing for Quality" included the creation of a new unit, the Public Competition and Purchasing Unit (PCPU). The new Unit has subsumed the work of the Central Unit on Purchasing (see page 116 of the 1990 Survey), but also has wider responsibilities to improve the effectiveness of market testing in government.

Regulatory review and reform

The booklet "Cutting Red Tape for Business", published in April 1991, reported progress on the Deregulation Initiative generally, together with a number of examples of deregulatory achievements. It also detailed the programme of work which will carry forward the Deregulation Initiative.

Supplementary reference material

Improving Management in Government: The Next Steps Agencies. HMSO, November 1991 (ISBN 0-10-117602-3).

Treasury and Civil Service Committee Report on Next Steps (HC496, Session 1990-91) and *the Government's response* (Cmnd 1761, November 1991). HMSO.

Making the Most of Next Steps: The Management of Ministers' Departments and their Executive Agencies. Efficiency Unit Report to the Prime Minister. HMSO, May 1991 (ISBN 0-11-430055-0).

Setting up Next Steps: A Short Account of the Origins, Launch and Implementation of the Next Steps Project in the British Civil Service. HMSO, May 1991 (ISBN 0-11-430056-9).

Office of the Minister for the Civil Service: A Force for Improvement in the UK Civil Service. Cabinet Office (OMCS), October 1991 (ISBN 0-7115-0223-4).

The Citizen's Charter. HMSO, July 1991 (ISBN 0-10-115992-7).

Competing for Quality: Buying Better Public Services. HMSO, November 1991 (ISBN 0-10-117302-4).

Achieving High Standards in Management: Applying the MCI Management Standards in the Workplace. Cabinet Office (OMCS), 1991 (ISBN 0-7115-019-12).

Developing People - The Line Manager's Job. Cabinet Office (OMCS), 1991.

Basic Issues of Training for Customer Service and Quality Management. Cabinet Office (OMCS), 1991.

Learning to Improve Customer Service. Cabinet Office (OMCS), 1990.

Young People Programme. Cabinet Office (OMCS), 1990.

Evaluating Training: A Manual. Cabinet Office (OMCS), 1989.

Equal Opportunities for Women in the Civil Service: Progress Report 1990. Cabinet Office (OMCS), 1990 (ISBN 0-11-430049-6).

Equal Opportunities for Women in the Civil Service: Progress Report 1990-91. Cabinet Office (OMCS), 1990 (ISBN 0-11-430060-7).

Programme for Action to Achieve Equality of Opportunity in the Civil Service for People of Ethnic Minority Origin. Cabinet Office (OMCS), 1990.

Equal Opportunities in the Civil Service for People of Ethnic Minority Origin: Progress Report 1990-91. Cabinet Office (OMCS), 1991 (ISBN 0-11-430059-3).

Cutting Red Tape for Business. Department of Trade and Industry, April 1991.

FACTSHEET: UNITED KINGDOM

A. PRINCIPAL RECENT PUBLIC MANAGEMENT DEVELOPMENTS

1979:
- Substantial range of measures launched to reduce the size of the state-controlled sector and to increase the proportion of privately-owned assets.

1981:
- Civil Service Department disbanded. Responsibilities transferred to Treasury and newly-formed Management and Personnel Office within the Cabinet Office.

1982:
- Financial Management Initiative introduced as a first step in a process of delegating financial and personnel management decision-making from the Treasury and Cabinet Office to line managers in departments.

1984:
- "Government Purchasing: Review of Government Contract and Procurement Procedures" published.
- Central Unit on Purchasing set up and charged with reporting annually on progress in achieving agreed value-for-money targets.

1985:
- White Paper "Lifting the Burden" spells out the need for deregulation.

1986:
- Multi-departmental Review of Budgeting completed including encouragement to develop budgeting as a management tool for improving resource allocation.
- White Paper "Building Business ... Not Barriers" published.

1987:
- Management and Personnel Office reconstituted as the Office of the Minister for the Civil Service (OMCS), giving support as part of the Cabinet Office to the Prime Minister.

1988:
- "Next Steps" initiative launched to promote the creation of Executive Agencies run by Chief Executives who are accountable to ministers who, in turn, set performance targets for them.
- Progress report on budgeting reforms published.
- White Paper "Releasing Enterprise" reports progress on deregulation and makes nearly 80 proposals for further action.

1989:
- Document issued by Treasury outlines 21 flexibilities available to departments or Agencies in the fields of personnel management, pay and allowances.
- New career arrangements for IT and Purchasing and Supply staff aimed at achieving greater professionalism.
- Further progress report on budget reforms indicates that one quarter of departments are still working to incorporate satisfactory output and performance measures into their budgetary systems.

1989/90:
- Challenge Funding introduced to improve the performance of departments in training senior managers.
- Flexible pay agreements now cover the majority of civil servants and provide for new pay structures and frameworks for determining pay.
- Range of measures introduced to develop a more flexible framework for recruitment, management development and training.
- Efficiency scrutinies and policy reviews continue.

1990:
- First annual review of "Next Steps" published with details of the targets and achievements to date of current Agencies.
- By October, 34 Agencies employing nearly 80 000 staff established and a further 29 potentially suitable candidates employing over 200 000 staff are identified.
- Series of equal opportunity initiatives launched including revision of Code of Practice for employing people with disabilities.

1991:
- By the end of 1991, 57 Agencies had been established and nearly 40 per cent of civil servants were working in organisations running on "Next Steps" lines.
- Publication of "Making the Most of Next Steps", a report by the Efficiency Unit on the relationship between departments and their Agencies.
- Second "Next Steps" annual review published.
- Publication of the "Citizen's Charter" White Paper.
- Publication of "Competing for Quality" White Paper, which requires departments to set targets for testing new areas of activity in the market. These targets will be published.
- Updated document issued by Treasury outlines 40 flexibilities available to departments or Agencies in the fields of personnel management, pay and allowances.
- Departments and Agencies to be allowed greater flexibilities and to establish their own pay and grading system.

B. INSTITUTIONAL RESPONSIBILITY FOR PUBLIC MANAGEMENT IMPROVEMENT

ORGANISATION	TASKS AND RESPONSIBILITIES	OTHER INFORMATION
Cabinet Office – Office of the Minister for the Civil Service	– implementation of the 'Next Steps' initiative – provides policy advice on the structure and practice of government – develops and promotes best practice and, through its three Agencies, provides services in staff recruitment and selection, staff development, and training and occupational health – promotes integrity, efficiency and merit (including equality of opportunity) throughout the Civil Service	The Cabinet Office (OMCS) and the Treasury share responsibility for the general principles and the necessary central machinery for the management of the Civil Service. Most management is, however, carried out by departments and Agencies.
– Citizen's Charter Unit (CCU)	– co-ordinates work on the Citizen's Charter	
– Efficiency Unit	– carries out efficiency scrutinies across the Civil Service	
Her Majesty's Treasury	– financial management and government purchasing – Civil Service pay and superannuation – industrial relations – other pay-related aspects of personnel management	

UNITED STATES

Organisational and structural change

The Office of Federal Financial Management, headed by the Controller, was established within the Office of Management and Budget (OMB). The position of Deputy Director for Management at OMB was filled. Twenty-two of 23 major departments and agencies required to have a Chief Financial Officer have now submitted and received OMB approval of their Chief Financial Officer re-organisation plans pursuant to the Chief Financial Officers Act (CFOs Act).

Better quality service delivery and client satisfaction

Federal and State governments are developing and testing Electronic Benefit Transfer (EBT) payment mechanisms. EBT delivers Federal and State benefits electronically through plastic cards, automatic teller machines at banks, and card-scanning devices in food stores. Demonstrations and planning are under way in many states, and, in 1991, state-wide use of EBT was approved for the State of Maryland following a successful demonstration.

Financial management

The first set of **annual audited financial statements** required by the CFOs Act were prepared. These statements were completed by three agencies and 27 Government corporations. An additional 70 entities will prepare statements in 1992. The financial statements cover financial and programme performance information, financial results and conditions, problems, and needs.

The **Federal Accounting Standards Advisory Board** (established in 1990) published proposed standards in three major areas. Standards covering additional areas are being prepared.

Quality improvement demonstrations were defined; they will assess and evaluate what particular efforts lead to higher quality service and products. These demonstrations will begin in 1992; they are associated with a rapidly growing emphasis on performance measurement. In 1991, several fact-finding and analytical efforts were begun. These are expected to lead to a more full-blown presentation of performance in 1992 and future years.

Human resource management

The **Federal Employees Pay Comparability Act** was enacted in November 1990. Among its major features are:
- a locality-based pay system that will reflect geographical variations in pay;
- special flexibilities, such as bonuses, that permit the Government to hire or retain individuals where there are difficult or unusual staffing problems; and
- a requirement to develop and institute systems that strengthen the link between pay and performance.

All three features were being implemented in 1991. For example, employees in three major metropolitan areas became the first to receive a locality-based pay differential.

Regulatory review and reform

For the regulatory programme developed for 1991, OMB asked Federal agencies to provide **cost and benefit data,** not just for "major" regulations, but for all significant regulations. ("Major" regulations are those likely to have an annual effect on the economy of $100 million or more.) This request increased the number of rules covered from about 80 to 500 per year. Cost and/or benefit estimates could not be provided for all significant regulations. Agencies have been more successful in providing cost information than benefit estimates, and they need to continue to improve their capabilities in the estimating area.

For several industrial sectors covered by 1990 Clean Air Act Amendments, a **pilot regulatory budget** is being tested by the Federal Government. Under such a "budget", a cap is being established for a set of technology-based standards governing industrial emissions. The Environmental Protection Agency will try to keep projected costs of meeting the standards below the budget cap.

Monitoring and evaluation

Agency reporting and tracking of progress under the **Management by Objectives** system was discontinued in 1991. This system tracked the implementation of selected major Federal Government initiatives and priorities.

Programme evaluation is defined as a formal assessment through objective measurement and systematic analysis of the manner, and extent, in which Federal Government programmes achieve intended objectives. Programme evaluation efforts in the Federal Government remain uneven. Few agencies perform results-oriented outcome evaluations. Process evaluations and related management analyses, such as compliance audits, are more usual. Such studies do not usually provide sufficient information by themselves to support major policy and budget allocation decisions. There is continued strong support for production of sound and timely programme evaluations.

FACTSHEET: UNITED STATES

A.   PRINCIPAL RECENT PUBLIC MANAGEMENT DEVELOPMENTS

1981:   –   Federal Government launches a major upgrade of financial management systems aimed at installing a single, government-wide financial system to replace the existing obsolescent central budget systems.

1984:   –   Simplification efforts include cutting 30 000 pages from the Federal Acquisition Regulation.

1986:   –   Launch of an extensive effort to improve the quality of government services and products, thereby improving efficiency and productivity.

1988:   –   Great increase in the number of agencies having Inspectors General who are empowered to carry out audits and investigations, particularly of wasteful and inefficient practices.
–   Continued efforts to improve the management and administration of the Federal Government's lending programmes.
–   Number of government financial systems reduced from 379 in 1984 to 253, and the number of government personnel payroll systems cut from 132 in 1983 to 53.
–   Significant progress reported in increasing the number of government contracts subjected to competition (from 41 per cent in 1981 to 58 per cent).

1989:   –   Major review across more than 65 departments and agencies of the adequacy of management controls.
–   Reviews of the development and use of IT in large systems and a focus on efforts to ensure appropriate confidentiality of data, data protection and streamlining of the contracting process.
–   Overview made of broad issues for programme emphasis into the next century, including initial long-range assessment of factors that could affect future government priorities, programmes and organisations.
–   Studies begun to identify actions to ensure that the Government continues to hire and retain skilled personnel.
–   A Management by Objectives system established to allow the President and senior officials to monitor and evaluate some 50 major programmes and policies.

1990:   –   The President signs into law a comprehensive federal pay reform measure affecting over 1.4 million federal civil employees linking federal salaries to those paid to comparable workers in local labour markets and giving managers greater flexibility to recruit and reward performance.
–   New legislation signed by the President to establish a formal integrated structure for financial management activities requiring goal-setting, preparation of annual financial statements, and the Presidential appointment of a Chief Financial Officer in 23 agencies.
–   New budget deficit reduction law revises rules to enforce budget deficit targets and sets discretionary spending caps for fiscal years 1991-93.
–   Pace of programme evaluation activity starts to accelerate.

1991:   –   Increased emphasis assigned to measurement of programme performance.
–   Implementation of the Chief Financial Officers Act, including establishing an Office of Federal Financial Management in the Office of Management and Budget, and publication of guidelines and standards for financial reporting and financial accounting.
–   Initial set of annual audited financial statements published by several agencies and 27 government corporations.
–   Renewed focus on improving quality of government services and products.
–   Tracking and reporting under the Management by Objectives system discontinued.

B. INSTITUTIONAL RESPONSIBILITY FOR PUBLIC MANAGEMENT IMPROVEMENT

ORGANISATION	TASKS AND RESPONSIBILITIES	OTHER INFORMATION
Executive Office of the President – Office of Management and Budget (OMB)	– assistance to the President in budget preparation and formulation of Government's fiscal programme – improvement of management and administration of government programmes – review of government regulations and rules affecting the public – overall guidance for government contracting policies, regulations and procedures – overall guidance for government financial management policies, including financial statements, financial systems, credit and cash management, and internal controls	
Office of Personnel Management (OPM)	– operation of federal employment system, including recruitment, testing, training and promotion – operation of civil service retirement and disability fund	Created in 1978 by the Civil Service Reform Act.
General Services Administration (GSA)	– policy and management of a system of property and records, construction and operation of government office and general purpose buildings, purchase of supplies, logistics and travel services, management of data processing services, and provision of telecommunications services	
Department of the Treasury – Financial Management Service (FMS)	– improving the management of government financial transactions – improving the management of government credit activities – issues Treasury checks and electronic fund transfers – maintains a central system of accounts with periodic reports on financial status – operates systems for collecting government receipts	

Annex

LIST OF NATIONAL CORRESPONDENTS
(as at 1.2.92)

Australia

Mr. Malcolm HOLMES
Principal Adviser
General Expenditure Division
Department of Finance
Newlands Street
Parkes, A.C.T. 2600

Austria

Mrs. Lieselotte RICHTER
Head of Division IV/7
Bundeskanzleramt (Federal Chancellery)
Ballhausplatz 2
A-1014 Vienna

Belgium

M. Jean-Marie MOTTOUL
Chef de Corps des Conseillers de
    la Fonction publique
Service d'Administration générale
Ministère de l'Intérieur et de la Fonction publique
19, boulevard Pachéco, Bte.2
B-1010 Bruxelles

Canada

Ms. Yvette ALOISI
Officer
Machinery of Government Secretariat
Privy Council Office
Langevin Block, Room 314
Ottawa, Ontario K1A 0A3

Denmark

Mr. Tommy JENSEN
Head of Section
Department of Management and Personnel
Finansministeriet (Ministry of Finance)
Bredgade 43
DK-1260 Copenhagen K

Finland

Mr. Markku KIVINIEMI
Research Manager
Valtionhallinnon kehittämiskeskus
(Administrative Development Agency)
P. L. 101
SF-00331 Helsinki

France

Mme Marie-Hélène POINSSOT
Sous Directeur de la modernisation et de la qualité
Direction générale de l'Administration
    et de la Fonction publique
Ministère de la Fonction publique et
    de la modernisation de l'Administration
32, rue de Babylone
F-75700 Paris

Germany

Dr. Dietmar SEILER
Director
Federal Academy of Public Administration
Federal Ministry of the Interior
Friedrich-Ebert-Strasse, 1
D-5300 Bonn 2

Greece

Mr. Vassilios ANDRONOPOULOS
Director-General
Ministry to the Presidency of Government
15, Vassilissis Sofias Avenue
GR-106 74 Athens

Iceland

Mr. Bolli HÉDINSSON
Economic Adviser to the Prime Minister
Prime Minister's Office
Stjornarradshusid
IS-150 Reykjavik

Ireland

Mr. Patrick J. MOORE
Assistant Secretary
Department of Finance
Agriculture House
Kildare Street
Dublin 2

Italy

Mr. Antonino VINCI
Director-General
Department of the Public Service
Presidency of the Council of Ministers
Palazzo Vidoni
Corso Vittorio Emanuele, 116
I-00186 Rome

Japan

Mr. Yoshihiro HIGUCHI
Second Secretary
Japanese Delegation to the OECD
7, avenue Hoche
F-75008 Paris FRANCE

Luxembourg

M. Pierre NEYENS
Directeur de l'Administration du Personnel de l'État
Ministère de la Fonction publique
L-2932 Luxembourg

Netherlands

Mrs. Diet VAN BORSELEN
Office of the Secretary General
Ministerie van Binnenlandse Zaken
 (Ministry of Home Affairs)
Postbus 20011
NL-2500 EA The Hague

New Zealand

Mr. David J. SWALLOW
Deputy State Services Commissioner
Office of the State Services Commission
100 Molesworth Street
P. O. Box 329
Wellington

Norway

Mr. Øystein S. LIEN
Deputy Director General
Ministry of Labour and Government Administration
Postboks 8004 DEP.
N-0030 Oslo

Portugal

Mrs. Maria Teresa SANCHES
Director General
Department of Project Evaluation
Ministry of Planning and Regional Development
Praça Duque de Saldanha, 31-4°
P-1000 Lisbon

Spain

Mr. Emilio CASALS PERALTA
Deputy Director for International Relations
Ministerio para las Administraciones Públicas
 (Ministry of Public Administration)
Paseo de la Castellana, 3
E-28046 Madrid

Sweden

Mr. Lennart ASPEGREN
Under-Secretary for Legal and International Affairs
Ministry of Public Administration
S-103 33 Stockholm

Switzerland

M. François COUCHEPIN
Chancelier de la Confédération Suisse
Chancellerie Fédérale
CH-3003 Berne

Turkey

Mrs. Reyyan ÖDEMIS
Head
Foreign Affairs Department
Prime Ministry
Bakanliklar
Ankara 06573

United Kingdom

Mr. Peter TALLANTIRE
The Next Steps Team
Cabinet Office (OMCS)
Horse Guards Road
London SW1P 3AL

United States

Mr. Franklin S. REEDER
Deputy Assistant Director for General Management
Office of Management and Budget
Executive Office of the President
725 17th Street, N.W.
Washington, D.C. 20503

Additional documents available on request
from the Public Management Service

Occasional Papers on Public Management:

Aspects of Managing the Centre of Government (May 1990)

Financing Public Expenditures through User Charges (May 1990)

Public Management and Private Enterprise: Administrative Responsiveness and the Needs of Small Firms (May 1990)

Performance Pay and Related Compensation Practices in Australian State Public Sector Organisations, by Robert Wood; **A Summary of the Experience with Pay for Performance in the United States,** by Patricia W. Ingraham (October 1991)

Serving the Economy Better (October 1991)

The United States Experience with Contracting Out under Circular A-76, by Larkin Sims Dudley; **The Case of User Charges for Prescription Drugs in Italy,** by Maurizio Ferrera; **Market-type Mechanisms and Health Services in the UK,** by Howard Glennerster (December 1991)

Public Management Service (PUMA)
OECD
2, rue André-Pascal
75775 Paris Cedex 16
France
Telefax: (33-1) 45.24.87.96

MAIN SALES OUTLETS OF OECD PUBLICATIONS
PRINCIPAUX POINTS DE VENTE DES PUBLICATIONS DE L'OCDE

ARGENTINA – ARGENTINE
Carlos Hirsch S.R.L.
Galería Güemes, Florida 165, 4° Piso
1333 Buenos Aires   Tel. (1) 331.1787 y 331.2391
                                    Telefax: (1) 331.1787

AUSTRALIA – AUSTRALIE
D.A. Book (Aust.) Pty. Ltd.
648 Whitehorse Road, P.O.B 163
Mitcham, Victoria 3132   Tel. (03) 873.4411
                                    Telefax: (03) 873.5679

AUSTRIA – AUTRICHE
Gerold & Co.
Graben 31
Wien I   Tel. (0222) 533.50.14

BELGIUM – BELGIQUE
Jean De Lannoy
Avenue du Roi 202
B-1060 Bruxelles   Tel. (02) 538.51.69/538.08.41
                                    Telefax: (02) 538.08.41

CANADA
Renouf Publishing Company Ltd.
1294 Algoma Road
Ottawa, ON K1B 3W8   Tel. (613) 741.4333
                                    Telefax: (613) 741.5439
Stores:
61 Sparks Street
Ottawa, ON K1P 5R1   Tel. (613) 238.8985
211 Yonge Street
Toronto, ON M5B 1M4   Tel. (416) 363.3171
Les Éditions La Liberté Inc.
3020 Chemin Sainte-Foy
Sainte-Foy, PQ G1X 3V6   Tel. (418) 658.3763
                                    Telefax: (418) 658.3763

Federal Publications
165 University Avenue
Toronto, ON M5H 3B8   Tel. (416) 581.1552
                                    Telefax: (416) 581.1743

CHINA – CHINE
China National Publications Import
Export Corporation (CNPIEC)
P.O. Box 88
Beijing   Tel. 403.5533
                                    Telefax: 401.5664

DENMARK – DANEMARK
Munksgaard Export and Subscription Service
35, Nørre Søgade, P.O. Box 2148
DK-1016 København K   Tel. (33) 12.85.70
                                    Telefax: (33) 12.93.87

FINLAND – FINLANDE
Akateeminen Kirjakauppa
Keskuskatu 1, P.O. Box 128
00100 Helsinki   Tel. (358 0) 12141
                                    Telefax: (358 0) 121.4441

FRANCE
OECD/OCDE
Mail Orders/Commandes par correspondance:
2, rue André-Pascal
75775 Paris Cedex 16   Tel. (33-1) 45.24.82.00
Telefax: (33-1) 45.24.85.00 or (33-1) 45.24.81.76
                                    Telex: 620 160 OCDE
OECD Bookshop/Librairie de l'OCDE :
33, rue Octave-Feuillet
75016 Paris   Tel. (33-1) 45.24.81.67
                                            (33-1) 45.24.81.81

Documentation Française
29, quai Voltaire
75007 Paris   Tel. 40.15.70.00

Gibert Jeune (Droit-Économie)
6, place Saint-Michel
75006 Paris   Tel. 43.25.91.19

Librairie du Commerce International
10, avenue d'Iéna
75016 Paris   Tel. 40.73.34.60

Librairie Dunod
Université Paris-Dauphine
Place du Maréchal de Lattre de Tassigny
75016 Paris   Tel. 47.27.18.56

Librairie Lavoisier
11, rue Lavoisier
75008 Paris   Tel. 42.65.39.95

Librairie L.G.D.J. - Montchrestien
20, rue Soufflot
75005 Paris   Tel. 46.33.89.85

Librairie des Sciences Politiques
30, rue Saint-Guillaume
75007 Paris   Tel. 45.48.36.02

P.U.F.
49, boulevard Saint-Michel
75005 Paris   Tel. 43.25.83.40

Librairie de l'Université
12a, rue Nazareth
13100 Aix-en-Provence   Tel. (16) 42.26.18.08

Documentation Française
165, rue Garibaldi
69003 Lyon   Tel. (16) 78.63.32.23

GERMANY – ALLEMAGNE
OECD Publications and Information Centre
Schedestrasse 7
D-W 5300 Bonn 1   Tel. (0228) 21.60.45
                                    Telefax: (0228) 26.11.04

GREECE – GRÈCE
Librairie Kauffmann
Mavrokordatou 9
106 78 Athens   Tel. 322.21.60
                                    Telefax: 363.39.67

HONG-KONG
Swindon Book Co. Ltd.
13–15 Lock Road
Kowloon, Hong Kong   Tel. 366.80.31
                                    Telefax: 739.49.75

ICELAND – ISLANDE
Mál Mog Menning
Laugavegi 18, Pósthólf 392
121 Reykjavik   Tel. 162.35.23

INDIA – INDE
Oxford Book and Stationery Co.
Scindia House
New Delhi 110001   Tel.(11) 331.5896/5308
                                    Telefax: (11) 332.5993
17 Park Street
Calcutta 700016   Tel. 240832

INDONESIA – INDONÉSIE
Pdii-Lipi
P.O. Box 4298
Jakarta 12042   Tel. 583467
                                    Telex: 62 875

IRELAND – IRLANDE
TDC Publishers – Library Suppliers
12 North Frederick Street
Dublin 1   Tel. 74.48.35/74.96.77
                                    Telefax: 74.84.16

ISRAEL
Electronic Publications only
Publications électroniques seulement
Sophist Systems Ltd.
71 Allenby Street
Tel-Aviv 65134   Tel. 3-29.00.21
                                    Telefax: 3-29.92.39

ITALY – ITALIE
Libreria Commissionaria Sansoni
Via Duca di Calabria 1/1
50125 Firenze   Tel. (055) 64.54.15
                                    Telefax: (055) 64.12.57
Via Bartolini 29
20155 Milano   Tel. (02) 36.50.83
Editrice e Libreria Herder
Piazza Montecitorio 120
00186 Roma   Tel. 679.46.28
                                    Telefax: 678.47.51
Libreria Hoepli
Via Hoepli 5
20121 Milano   Tel. (02) 86.54.46
                                    Telefax: (02) 805.28.86
Libreria Scientifica
Dott. Lucio de Biasio 'Aeiou'
Via Coronelli, 6
20146 Milano   Tel. (02) 48.95.45.52
                                    Telefax: (02) 48.95.45.48

JAPAN – JAPON
OECD Publications and Information Centre
Landic Akasaka Building
2-3-4 Akasaka, Minato-ku
Tokyo 107   Tel. (81.3) 3586.2016
                                    Telefax: (81.3) 3584.7929

KOREA – CORÉE
Kyobo Book Centre Co. Ltd.
P.O. Box 1658, Kwang Hwa Moon
Seoul   Tel. 730.78.91
                                    Telefax: 735.00.30

MALAYSIA – MALAISIE
Co-operative Bookshop Ltd.
University of Malaya
P.O. Box 1127, Jalan Pantai Baru
59700 Kuala Lumpur
Malaysia   Tel. 756.5000/756.5425
                                    Telefax: 755.4424

NETHERLANDS – PAYS-BAS
SDU Uitgeverij
Christoffel Plantijnstraat 2
Postbus 20014
2500 EA's-Gravenhage   Tel. (070 3) 78.99.11
Voor bestellingen: Tel. (070 3) 78.98.80
                                    Telefax: (070 3) 47.63.51

NEW ZEALAND
NOUVELLE-ZÉLANDE
Legislation Services
P.O. Box 12418
Thorndon, Wellington   Tel. (04) 496.5652
                                    Telefax: (04) 496.5698

NORWAY – NORVÈGE
Narvesen Info Center – NIC
Bertrand Narvesens vei 2
P.O. Box 6125 Etterstad
0602 Oslo 6   Tel. (02) 57.33.00
                                    Telefax: (02) 68.19.01

PAKISTAN
Mirza Book Agency
65 Shahrah Quaid-E-Azam
Lahore 3   Tel. 66.839
                    Telex: 44886 UBL PK. Attn: MIRZA BK

PORTUGAL
Livraria Portugal
Rua do Carmo 70-74
Apart. 2681
1117 Lisboa Codex   Tel.: (01) 347.49.82/3/4/5
                                    Telefax: (01) 347.02.64

SINGAPORE – SINGAPOUR
Information Publications Pte
Golden Wheel Bldg.
41, Kallang Pudding, #04-03
Singapore 1334   Tel. 741.5166
                              Telefax: 742.9356

SPAIN – ESPAGNE
Mundi-Prensa Libros S.A.
Castelló 37, Apartado 1223
Madrid 28001   Tel. (91) 431.33.99
                              Telefax: (91) 575.39.98

Librería Internacional AEDOS
Consejo de Ciento 391
08009 – Barcelona   Tel. (93) 488.34.92
                              Telefax: (93) 487.76.59
Llibreria de la Generalitat
Palau Moja
Rambla dels Estudis, 118
08002 – Barcelona
              (Subscripcions) Tel. (93) 318.80.12
              (Publicacions) Tel. (93) 302.67.23
                              Telefax: (93) 412.18.54

SRI LANKA
Centre for Policy Research
c/o Colombo Agencies Ltd.
No. 300-304, Galle Road
Colombo 3   Tel. (1) 574240, 573551-2
                   Telefax: (1) 575394, 510711

SWEDEN – SUÈDE
Fritzes Fackboksföretaget
Box 16356
Regeringsgatan 12
103 27 Stockholm   Tel. (08) 23.89.00
                              Telefax: (08) 20.50.21

Subscription Agency-Agence d'abonnements
Wennergren-Williams AB
Nordenflychtsvägen 74
Box 30004
104 25 Stockholm   Tel. (08) 13.67.00
                              Telefax: (08) 618.62.32

SWITZERLAND – SUISSE
Maditec S.A. (Books and Periodicals - Livres
et périodiques)
Chemin des Palettes 4
1020 Renens/Lausanne   Tel. (021) 635.08.65
                              Telefax: (021) 635.07.80

Mail orders only - Commandes
par correspondance seulement
Librairie Payot
C.P. 3212
1002 Lausanne   Telefax: (021) 311.13.92

Librairie Unilivres
6, rue de Candolle
1205 Genève   Tel. (022) 320.26.23
                              Telefax: (022) 329.73.18

Subscription Agency - Agence d'abonnement
Naville S.A.
38 avenue Vibert
1227 Carouge   Tél.: (022) 308.05.56/57
                              Telefax: (022) 308.05.88

See also – Voir aussi :
OECD Publications and Information Centre
Schedestrasse 7
D-W 5300 Bonn 1 (Germany)
                              Tel. (49.228) 21.60.45
                              Telefax: (49.228) 26.11.04

TAIWAN – FORMOSE
Good Faith Worldwide Int'l. Co. Ltd.
9th Floor, No. 118, Sec. 2
Chung Hsiao E. Road
Taipei   Tel. (02) 391.7396/391.7397
                  Telefax: (02) 394.9176

THAILAND – THAÏLANDE
Suksit Siam Co. Ltd.
113, 115 Fuang Nakhon Rd.
Opp. Wat Rajbopith
Bangkok 10200   Tel. (662) 251.1630
                              Telefax: (662) 236.7783

TURKEY – TURQUIE
Kültur Yayinlari Is-Türk Ltd. Sti.
Atatürk Bulvari No. 191/Kat. 13
Kavaklidere/Ankara   Tel. 428.11.40 Ext. 2458
Dolmabahce Cad. No. 29
Besiktas/Istanbul   Tel. 160.71.88
                              Telex: 43482B

UNITED KINGDOM – ROYAUME-UNI
HMSO
Gen. enquiries   Tel. (071) 873 0011
Postal orders only:
P.O. Box 276, London SW8 5DT
Personal Callers HMSO Bookshop
49 High Holborn, London WC1V 6HB
                              Telefax: (071) 873 8200
Branches at: Belfast, Birmingham, Bristol, Edin-
burgh, Manchester

UNITED STATES – ÉTATS-UNIS
OECD Publications and Information Centre
2001 L Street N.W., Suite 700
Washington, D.C. 20036-4910 Tel. (202) 785.6323
                              Telefax: (202) 785.0350

VENEZUELA
Libreria del Este
Avda F. Miranda 52, Aptdo. 60337
Edificio Galipán
Caracas 106   Tel. 951.1705/951.2307/951.1297
                  Telegram: Libreste Caracas

YUGOSLAVIA – YOUGOSLAVIE
Jugoslovenska Knjiga
Knez Mihajlova 2, P.O. Box 36
Beograd   Tel. (011) 621.992
                              Telefax: (011) 625.970

Orders and inquiries from countries where Distribu-
tors have not yet been appointed should be sent to:
OECD Publications Service, 2 rue André-Pascal,
75775 Paris Cedex 16, France.

Les commandes provenant de pays où l'OCDE n'a
pas encore désigné de distributeur devraient être
adressées à : OCDE, Service des Publications,
2, rue André-Pascal, 75775 Paris Cedex 16, France.

Subscription to OECD periodicals may also be
placed through main subscription agencies.

Les abonnements aux publications périodiques de
l'OCDE peuvent être souscrits auprès des
principales agences d'abonnement.

OECD PUBLICATIONS, 2 rue André-Pascal, 75775 PARIS CEDEX 16
PRINTED IN FRANCE
(42 92 01 1) ISBN 92-64-13729-7 - No. 46089 1992